EXOTIC SCALES AND ARPEGGIOS

Bryan DeLauney

A special thanks to http://jguitar.com for allowing me to use their scale and arpeggio diagrams and chord charts!!
Go visit their site, its great!!

CONTENTS

Contents

ACKNOWLEDGMENTS

I'd like to thank all of the people that have helped me along the way and those who have believed in me. Thanks to my dear and lovely wife for all of her support. Thanks above all to my Lord and Savior, Jesus Christ!

Chapter 1 – *Introduction*

I can remember the first time that I heard Yngwie Malmsteen playing over my stereo and thinking it was the greatest thing ever. He played heavy metal (well, it was considered metal in those days) with a classical twist. Yngwie still blazes over the guitar inspiring young and old musicians, still today.

What makes him so inspirational is that he plays music using scales and ideas that are not conventional in today's music. Most guitarists know enough music to be dangerous, at best. They learn the first scale that everyone in the world learns and they think that they are fantastic, because they can memorize a TAB solo to *Sanitarium*, or they can play *Knocking on Heaven's Door*.

What Malmsteen was playing was the norm for the Classical or Baroque period. His solos are laced with melodic minor, harmonic minor, natural minor scales, and modes. He also adds in arpeggios to boot. Everyone wanted to be Yngwie, in the 80s.

In the 90s, people still wanted to be Yngwie, but a couple new guys came around that got people's attention; one was Marty Friedman. He played with the lesser known at the time, Jason Becker, in a band called *Cacophony*. This band played metal twisted with the same type of scales and arpeggios, but they added a new element into the mix, exotic scales.

A lot of what they did, especially Marty Friedman, was play four or five note scales mainly for the sound as opposed to any scale that was out. I've seen a Marty Friedman guitar lesson video and much of what he talked about was playing what sound he wanted to come out of the guitar. He never talked about scales that he used or memorized.

This isn't to say that everyone can do that. Many of us have to study hard and think about what we want to do, rather than just play what we want to, when we want to. This book is comprised of the theory behind many of the exotic scales and arpeggios that are used today. How to and where to used them always seems to be the fun part of music. You'll be surprised in how you can change the sound of an entire passage, by playing something out of the box.

My books that I write are not a fanciful way to regurgitate the same old garbage that you couldn't understand before. I am writing about how I learned this with a pencil and a sheet of paper. This is how I memorized things and looked at them from a human perspective. This is the real deal when it comes to theory and how to understand it. I have read through college music theory text books and they contain the same information that I present to you; just in a real language that you can understand.

This book isn't about trying to look brilliant. I am not trying to impress the musical intellects that have their proverbial noses in the air, snubbing all of us unlearned peasants. I want the regular Joe/Josephina, who sits on his/her bed and wants to learn how to really play music, and understand it. I will write just like I am now to you, and I will write something stupid to help you learn it, or say something completely corny so that you won't be so bored and want to give up, and I will hopefully teach you something about music.

Here is the rest of the speech:

Theory takes away the guesswork in music. There is too much information in music for one to just store it in virtual memory. When there are so many different scales and modes, it helps to refer back to a piece of paper to visualize things. The vision helps to lock things into memory and writing things down is also a memory tool. Use a pen and paper… For real; no joke.

Now let's talk about music. I do understand that most people will brush over the introduction like it is a waste of time, and get on with the cool stuff, but just give me a minute to get the ball rolling. Use this book as a reference, guide, tool, kindling, torch, I don't care really. But, if you want to get something out of music you need to know that music is not how many notes you can play a second, it's not how cool you are, it isn't how smart you are, nor is it how many scales you can memorize.

Music is in the mind, it is a rhythm, a melody. All of the scales in the world will make you a better nobody, but using one scale wisely will make you a star. Practice hard and study hard. When you start a new section, understand it fully before you move on. When you play a new scale or mode, don't just memorize it and move to the next one. Put on a jam track and try to use it. Integrate it into your playing and go from one scale that you know into the new scale you just learned. Do that before you move on and it will come together more smoothly.

I am not going to teach you what a bend is or how to tune your guitar. This isn't a fundamentals in guitar book. I don't intend on writing tons of "licks".

This book is not intended to be a standalone, learn it all, and know everything kind of book. There is so much involved in music theory that people get doctorates in the subject. There is no way I can cover that level in one book. This book should coincide either with prior knowledge and/or lessons. Take your time. You don't have to read this book in a day. Take small bites, work hard, study, use your pen and paper, ask your instructor or someone who knows (email a music professor) if you have questions, and enjoy yourself. You play a guitar not work a guitar. Make it fun.

Ok. I get the question on if I have the knowledge, how do I apply it. The key to knowledge is understanding it. Having knowledge is useless unless you understand the knowledge you possess.

Take the time to see the relationships between scales, keys, chords, etc. How do these chords relate? How do these three chords in this chord pattern relate to the notes in the scale playing over them? The take home lesson here is relationships. Look at the notes. Compare notes in chords. Compare notes in scales. Compare notes from scales to chords.

Let's get started learning!!!

Chapter 2 – *Natural Minor, Harmonic Minor, and Phrygian Dominant*

These concepts are constructed under the impression that you understand intervals and major scales. If you read this and are in need of a refresher, or you haven't learned those concepts, get either my *Interval and Major Scale Theory* book or *A Guitarist's Guide to Theory*. Don't get frustrated because you don't want to learn the basics. You may be a great guitar player, but our goal is to be a great musician, and if you went to college to get a degree in music, you'd have to take the basics. It's nothing to be ashamed of.

What are exotic scales? What makes them exotic? Many of the scales that are considered "exotic" are played or were played in lesser known parts of the world, or they were played mainly in small areas, and not anywhere else. If you traveled to India and listened to a street musician, you are more than likely not going to hear them playing I-IV-V in the key of G. What they'd be playing would seem strange and exotic to you, but seem absolutely normal to them.

The *common practice period* is the Baroque, Classical, and Romantic periods which was foundational in the creation of Western music and is now the conventional way to look at music. I am going to give you a few tables as a reminder.

Table 2-1:

Root		M2		M3		P4		P5		M6		M7		8va
	W		W		H		W		W		W		H	
C		D		E		F		G		A		B		C

Table 2-1 shows the major scale in the key of C. All of the scales from here on out will be explained in relation to the major scale or a mode of the major scale. This is so we can have a reference point. We can't explain how it's different unless we have something to compare it to.

When comparing minor scales, we will usually compare it to the A natural minor, and when comparing major scales we will compare it to the C major scale.

HARMONIC MINOR:

Let's start with the harmonic minor scale. The harmonic minor is one of the most used of the exotic scales; it and the Phrygian dominant scale. This scale has also been referred to as the Mohammedan scale. Lets look at the natural minor scale and then the harmonic minor scale.

Table 2-2:

A		B		C		D		E		F		G		A
	W		H		W		W		H		W		W	

A Natural Minor Scale

Table 2-3:

A		B		C		D		E		F		G#		A
	W		H		W		W		H		WH		H	

A Harmonic minor scale

By quick observation of the notes we can see that the A harmonic minor has a G# where the A natural minor has a G. Also by looking at the step progression we can see that the harmonic minor has a 1 ½ step (WH) followed by a half step (H), where the natural minor has a whole step (W) followed by a W. Simple math tells us that 1 ½ + ½ = 2; which is equal to the 2 whole steps of the natural minor scale.

This means that in the second tetrachord (also called the upper tetrachord) there is a W-H in the harmonic minor scale where there is a W-W in the natural minor scale. Let's look at the tetrachords for a refresher.

Table 2-4:

Name	Steps	Bottom Degree	Upper Degree	Bottom Example	Upper Example
Major	W-W-H	1-2-3-4	5-6-7-8	C-D-E-F	G-A-B-C
Minor	W-H-W	1-2-b3-4	5-6-b7-8	C-D-Eb-F	G-A-Bb-C
Phrygian	H-W-W	1-b2-b3-4	5-b6-b7-8	C-Db-Eb-F	G-Ab-Bb-C
Gypsy	H-WH-H	1-b2-3-4	5-b6-7-8	C-Db-E-F	G-Ab-B-C

Remember that the common precept is that we have two tetrachords separated by a whole step.

The natural minor is a minor bottom and Phrygian upper tetrachord combination.

W-H-W   W   H-W-W.

The harmonic minor is a minor bottom and a Gypsy (aka, harmonic tetrachord) upper tetrachord combination.

W-H-W   W   H-WH-H

If we put this in the format of degrees:

-Natural minor: 1-2-b3-4-5-b6-b7

-Harmonic minor: 1-2-b3-4-5-b6-7

Intervals of natural minor: P1-M2-m3-P4-P5-m6-m7

Intervals of harmonic minor: P1-M2-m3-P4-P5-m6-M7

So, in essence, this is the same thing as the natural minor but with a M7 (instead of a m7). This minor change will affect the chords that are created by the scale; which will change what you can play it over. Next we'll look at the chords created from both scales. If you don't understand what we are doing here, get my *A Guitarist's Guide to Theory* or any of my books that may expand on the fundamental areas that you are lacking in.

Table 2-5:

A Natural Minor Modes	Triad Name	Seven Chord Name
A-B-C-D-E-F-G-A	Am	Am7
B-C-D-E-F-G-A-B	Bdim	Bm7b5
C-D-E-F-G-A-B-C-	C major	Cm7
D-E-F-G-A-B-C-D	Dm	Dm7
E-F-G-A-B-C-D-E	Em	Em7
F-G-A-B-C-D-E-F	F major	Fmaj7
G-A-B-C-D-E-F-G	G major	G7

The chords that are created from the A natural minor should be of no surprise, because the A natural minor is actually a mode of the C major scale called the Aeolian mode. All major scales have the same chord progression created from their notes. This is what I call my Major Scale Chord Mantra.

Major Scale Chord Mantra:

Major-minor-minor-Major-Major-minor-diminished

Then of course if we reorganize the mantra, starting at the sixth note, we get:

minor-diminished-Major-minor-minor-Major-Major

Just like Table 2-5 shows. You can play the A natural minor over any C major or Am chord progression, G major (Em) chord progression that excludes the Bm, D major, or F#dim chords. You can overlook these scales if you are smart in either your chord creation or you can play the natural minor on top of the chords that fit and move to another scale on the chords that don't fit. As a side note, in the major scale the diminished chords are really half diminished.

This is what I do. This is why I play out of the G major so much. There are so many chord progressions that have G, Am, Bm, C, D, and Em in them that I can float in and out of the G major (or any mode in G major) and connect it with other scales and arpeggios that work in the chords that don't fit. This allows you to be really proficient in one scale and marginally proficient in others and sound like a king. Yngwie Malmsteen plays almost exclusively in Am, for this reason.

Try substitutions for the chords that don't fit like I have below, to begin with. This will allow you to play exclusively in a scale while learning it and not having to walk in and out of the scale, until you have it locked in your muscle memory.

In the key of G major (Em) substitute chords to make it work – Bm no 5, Bm7 no 5, D5, Dsus2 or Dsus4. You can always skip the chords entirely if you wish, but by doing so it isn't any different than playing in the key of C major or A minor. The objective is not to play the F# that is not in the A natural minor. Of course, you can play the E natural minor in the key of G, because (wait for it) it's the E Aeolian mode that is in the key of G major.

This isn't about the natural minor scale, but we are laying down a foundation as a comparison that will carry forward in subsequent chapters, but by then we will forego the chit-chat, because we discussed it here.

List of chords to play A natural minor scale over:

Am, Bm7b5, C major, Dm, Em, F major, G major

A, C, D, E, F, G: 5 chords (power chords), Sus2 and Sus4 chords

Am7, CM7, Dm7, Em7, FM7, G7, Cadd9, Fadd9, Gadd9

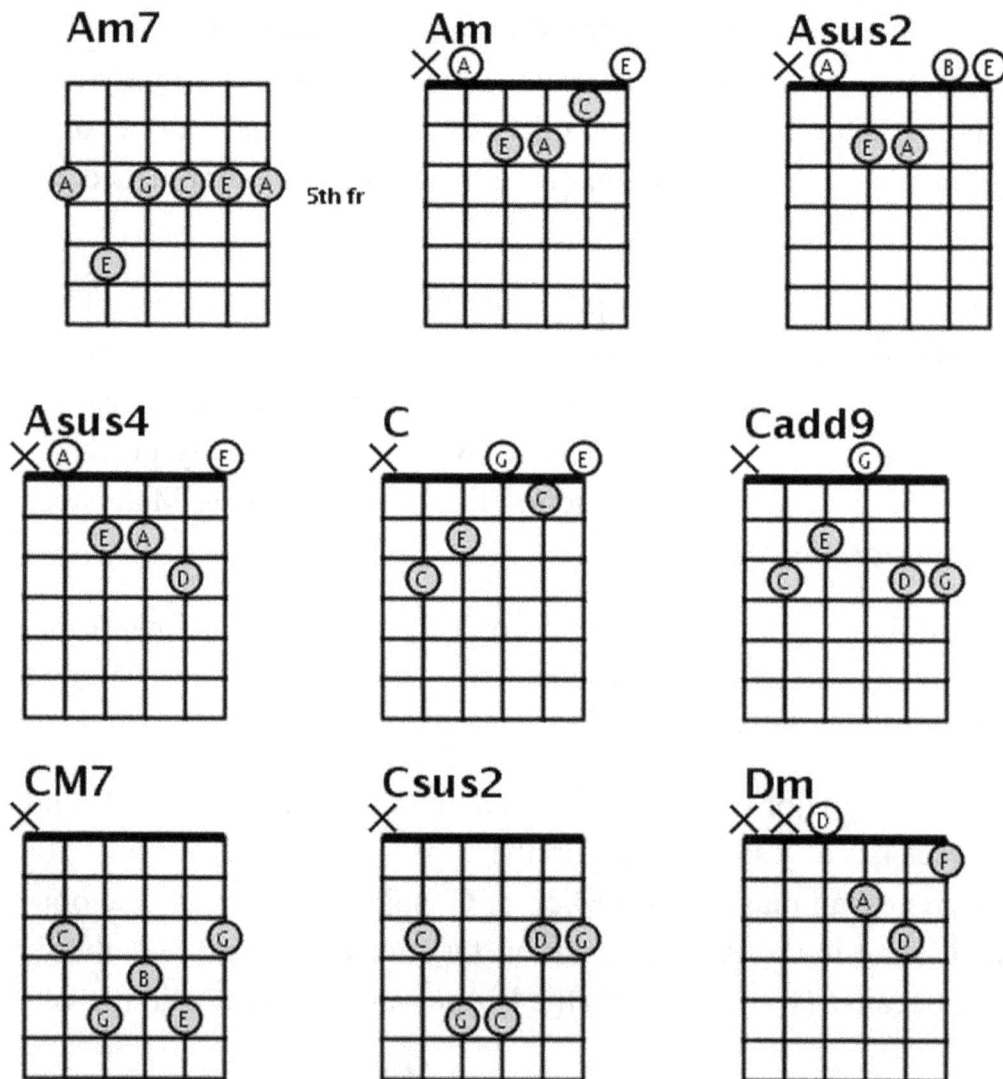

Am7   Am   Asus2

Asus4   C   Cadd9

CM7   Csus2   Dm

Dm7
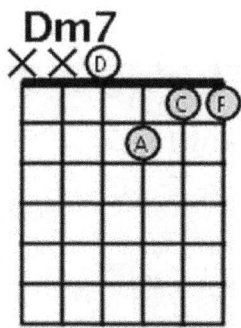

Dsus2
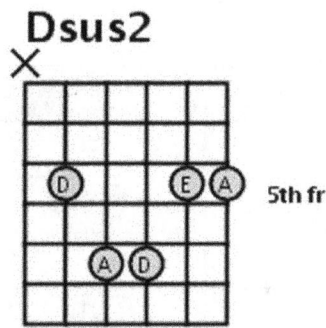

5th fr

Em7
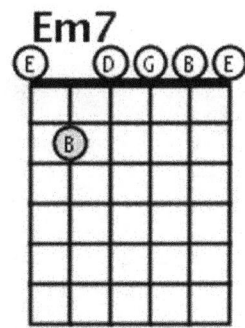

Em
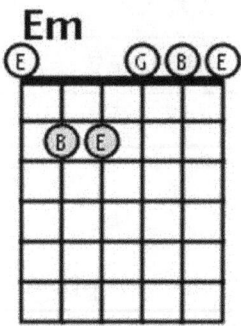

Esus4
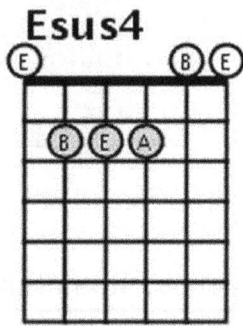

F
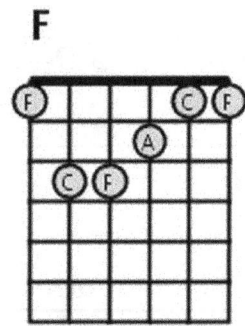

Fsus2
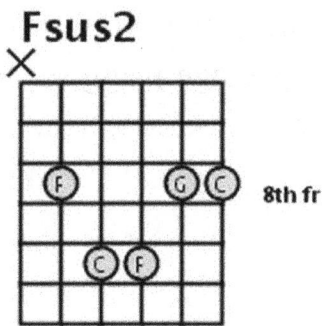

8th fr

G7
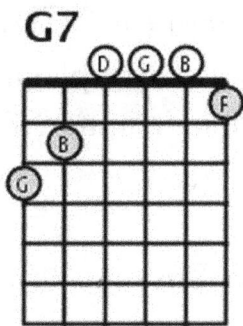

G
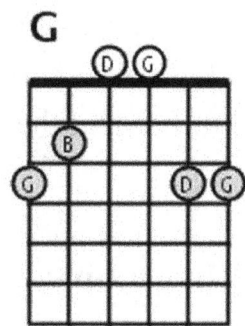

Gsus2
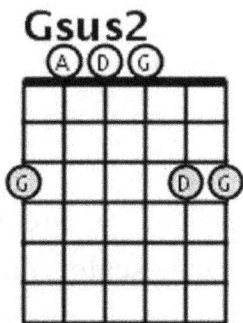

Table 2-6:

A Harmonic Minor Modes	Triad Name	Seventh Chord Name
A-B-C-D-E-F-G#-A	Am	Am(maj7)
B-C-D-E-F-G#-A-B	Bm	Bm7b5
C-D-E-F-G#-A-B-C	C+	C+M7
D-E-F-G#-A-B-C-D	Dm	Dm7
E-F-G#-A-B-C-D-E	E major	E7
F-G#-A-B-C-D-E-F	F major	Fmaj7
G#-A-B-C-D-E-F-G#	G#°	G#°7

The harmonic minor is used to correct the natural minor's i-iv-v progression. When you play the natural minor's i-iv-v progression, there is a touch of tension on the v chord. By raising the third and making a V chord (major not minor), the progression has better harmony, hence the name harmonic minor. Try playing a passage using the 1-4-5 chords from the natural minor and then the harmonic minor. Two progressions in Am are below.

Natural Minor: i-iv-v = Am-Dm-Em

Harmonic Minor: i-iv-V = Am-Dm-E

The chords built out of the natural minor are identical to that of the major scale. That's because they are essentially the same scale. You will notice that the E major chord at the end of the harmonic minor progression sounds more harmonious. This is where you will see the use of the harmonic minor scale the most. The song or passage will utilize the major V chord in the place of the minor v chord, opening up the perfect opportunity for the harmonic minor.

Let's do some side by side comparisons of the two scales.

Table 2-7:

A Natural Minor Triad/Seven Chord	A Harmonic Minor Triad/Seven Chord
Am/Am7	Am/Am(maj7)
Bdim/Bm7b5	Bdim/Bm7b5
C major/CM7	C+/Cmaj7#5
Dm/Dm7	Dm/Dm7
Em/Em7	E major/E7
F major/FM7	F major/FM7
G major/G7	G#dim/G#°7

The chords built from the other minors (why anyone would make a chord progression from this scale is beyond me) are a bit more interesting than from the natural minor. Note: there are no melodic minor or harmonic minor keys. They share the same key signature as the natural minor scale, but you can make chords from them if you wish.

The harmonic minor is pretty well known for being a "classical" sounding scale. It has very interesting properties as we described above. Below, Figures 2-1 and 2-2 show the notes and their positions on the fretboard. The key is to find comfortable positions. They don't necessarily need to be 3 notes per string either. Try starting on different As, sliding forward, or going down to the next string instead of forward to the next fret; just to name a few ideas.

Figure 2-1:

A Aeolian

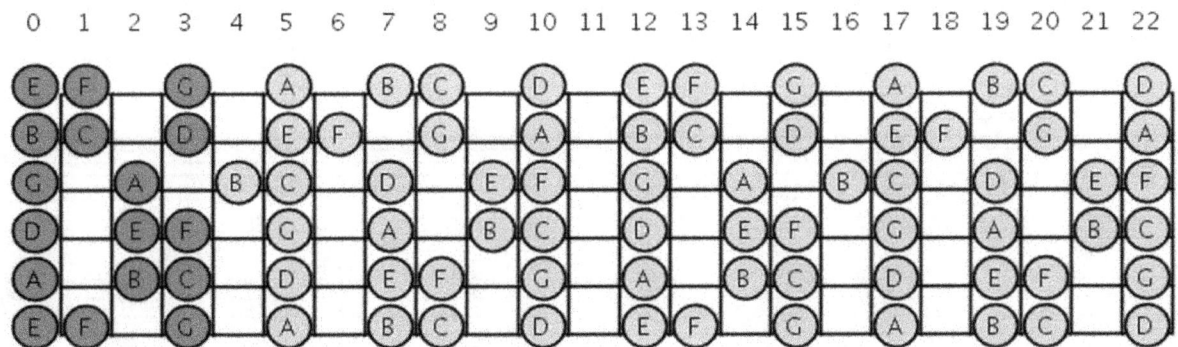

A Aeolian / A natural minor

The A natural minor should be as easy as playing the major scale, but starting on the 6th degree, instead of the 1st.

Tab 2-1: A Natural Minor

Gtr I A B C D E F G A B C D E F G A

Tab 2-2: C Major

Gtr I C D E F G A B C D E F G A B C

Tab 2-3: C major phrase

Tab 2-4: A natural minor phrase

Figure 2-2:

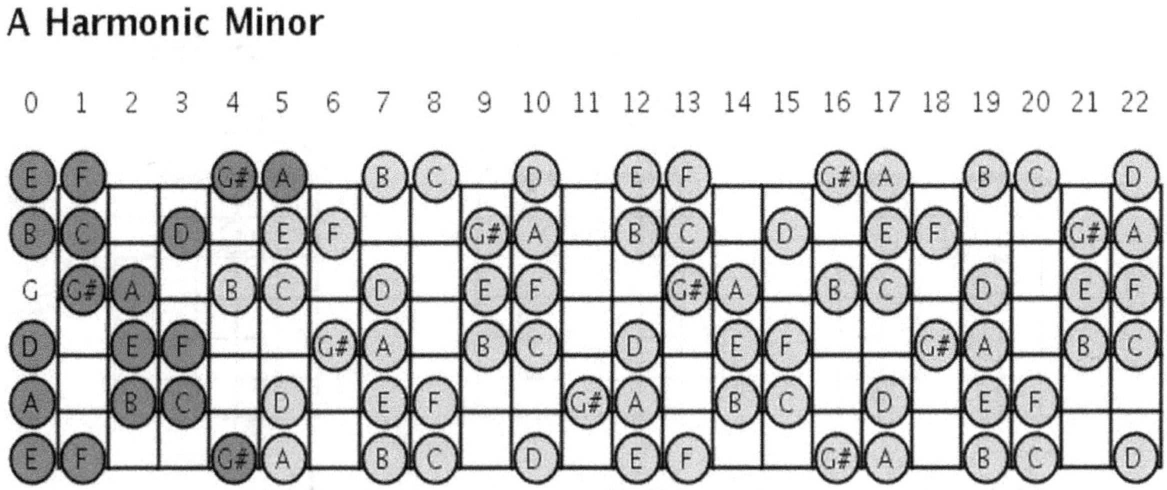

A Harmonic Minor

The A harmonic minor, on the other hand has this WH step in it that makes it have huge leaps. Some people have long fingers and this is no big deal, but most of us have normal sized hands and that jump isn't easy to do unless it is strategically placed by putting it on a different string, or using slides to your advantage.

List of chords to play A harmonic minor scale over:

E major, F major, Dm, Fm, Am, D5, E5, F5, A5

Dsus2, Asus2, Esus4, Asus4

E7, Dm7, Fm(maj7), FM7, Am(maj7), Dm7b5, Bm7b5, Bdim

E7
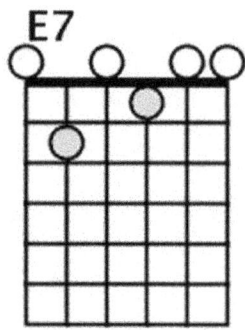

E
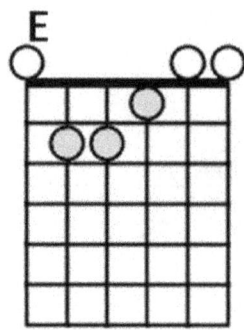

Esus4
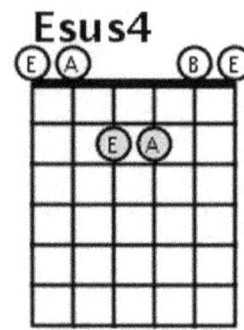

F
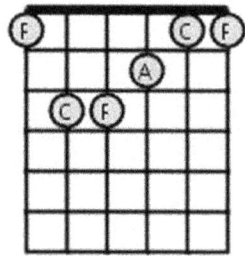

FmM7
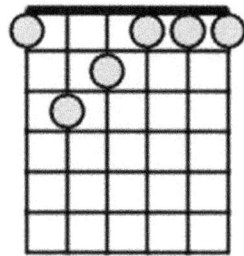

Fm
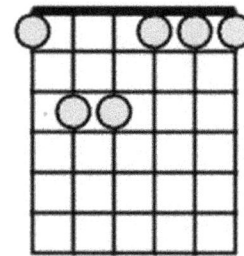

FmM7
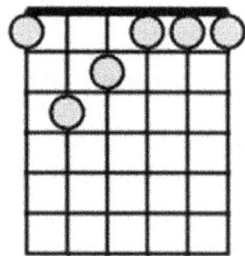

Am
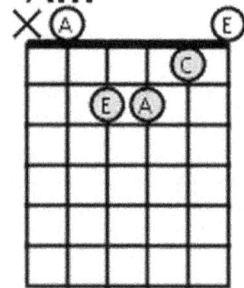

Asus2
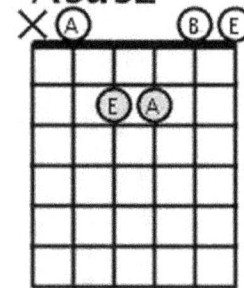

Asus4
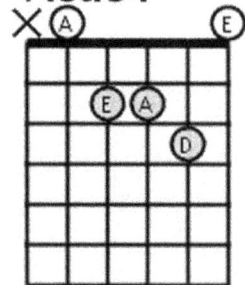

Bdim
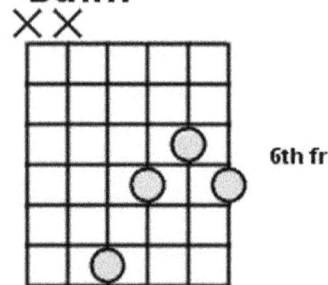

6th fr

Dm
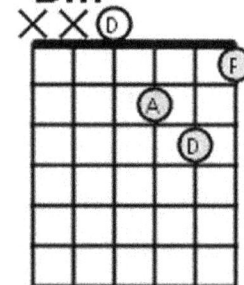

Dm7 **Dsus2**

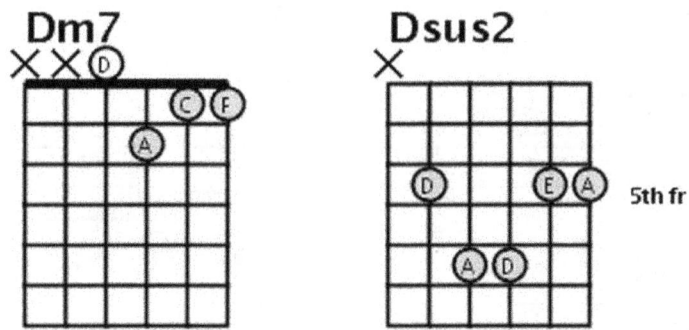

Tab 2-5: A Harmonic minor

Gtr I   A   B   C   D   E   F   G#   A   B   C   D   E   F   G#   A

Tab 2-6: A Harmonic minor ascending with slide

Gtr I   A   B   C   D   E   F   G#   A   B   C   D   E   F   G#   A

Tab 2-7: A Harmonic minor descending with slides

Tab 2-8: A Harmonic minor phrase

PHRYGIAN DOMINANT:

The harmonic minor has a famous mode (they all have modes) that gets used quite a bit in the neoclassical metal genre. This is the Phrygian dominant scale. It is also referred to as the Spanish Phrygian, AhavaRabbah, Freygish, Jewish scale, Nahawand-Hijaz (say that 3 times backwards), and who knows what else.

It is essentially the 5th mode of the harmonic minor scale.

Where the A harmonic minor would read:

A-B-C-D-E-F-G#

The Phrygian dominant scale is:

E-F-G#-A-B-C-D

It is called a dominant scale because it is a major scale (M3, G#) with a b7 (D). This is the characteristic of a dominant scale.

The Phrygian dominant is a Gypsy bottom and Phrygian upper tetrachord combination.

H-WH-H   W   H-W-W

-Phrygian dominant: 1-b2-3-4-5-b6-b7

-Phrygian mode: 1-b2-b3-4-5-b6-b7

Intervals of Phrygian dominant: P1-m2-M3-P4-P5-m6-m7

Intervals of Phrygian mode: P1-m2-m3-P4-P5-m6-m7

As you can see the Phrygian dominant is a Major type of scale. This can be seen by looking at the 3rd degree of the scale. The Phrygian mode is minor, but the Phrygian dominant is major. As explained before a seven chord built out of the progression gives us E-G#-B-D, which is an E7 chord (dominant seven chord).

Tab 2-8: E Phrygian dominant chords

Figure 2-3:

E Phrygian Dominant

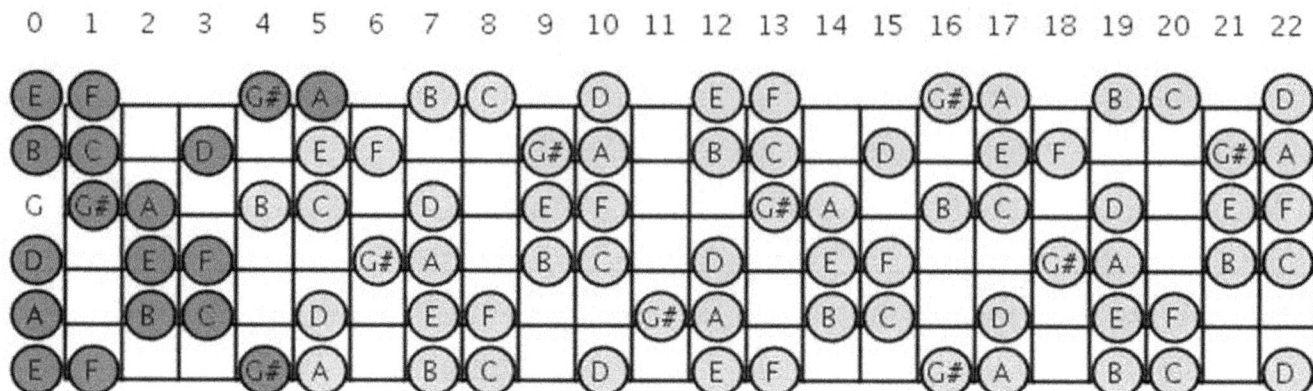

The tricky thing here, just like in the harmonic minor, is the WH leaps. This can be overcome in the same manner as mentioned previously.

Tab 2-9: E Phrygian dominant scale with slides

GtrI E F G# A B C D E   F G# A B C D E F   G# A B C

Tab 2-10: E Phrygian scale descending with slides

GtrI C B A G# F E D C   B A G# F E D C B   A G# F E

Tab 2-11: E Phrygian phrase

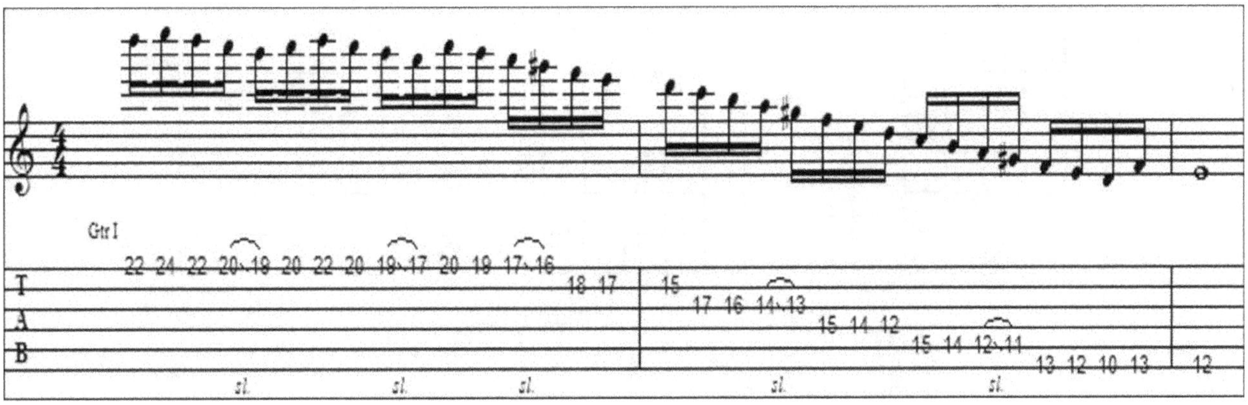

List of chords to play A Phrygian dominant scale over:

E major, F major, Dm, Fm, Am, D5, E5, A5, F5

Dsus2, Asus2, Esus4, Asus4

E7, Dm7, FM7, Dm7b5, Bm7b5

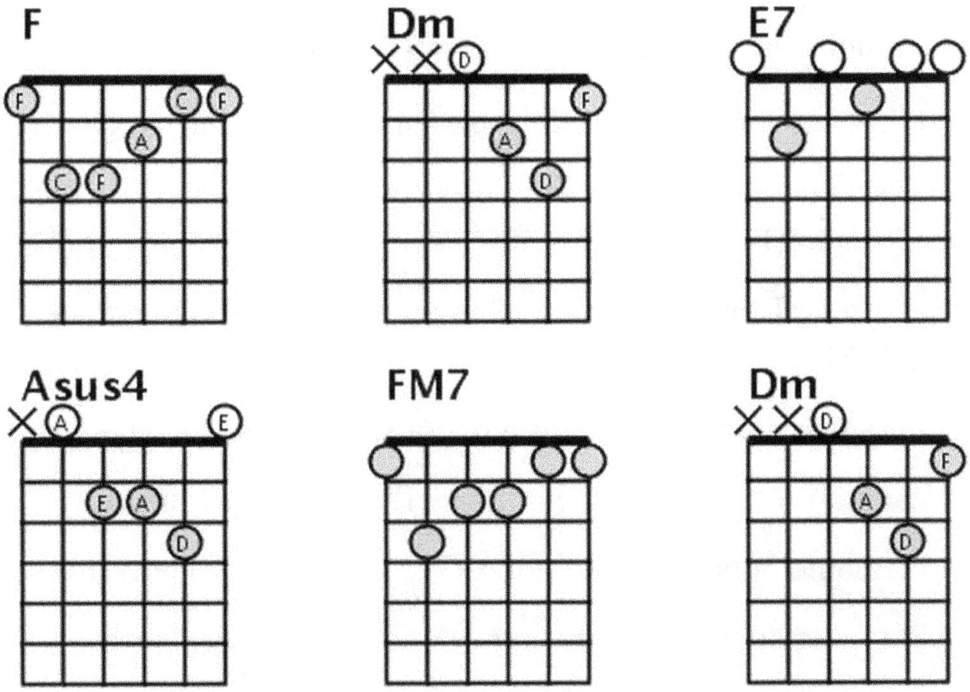

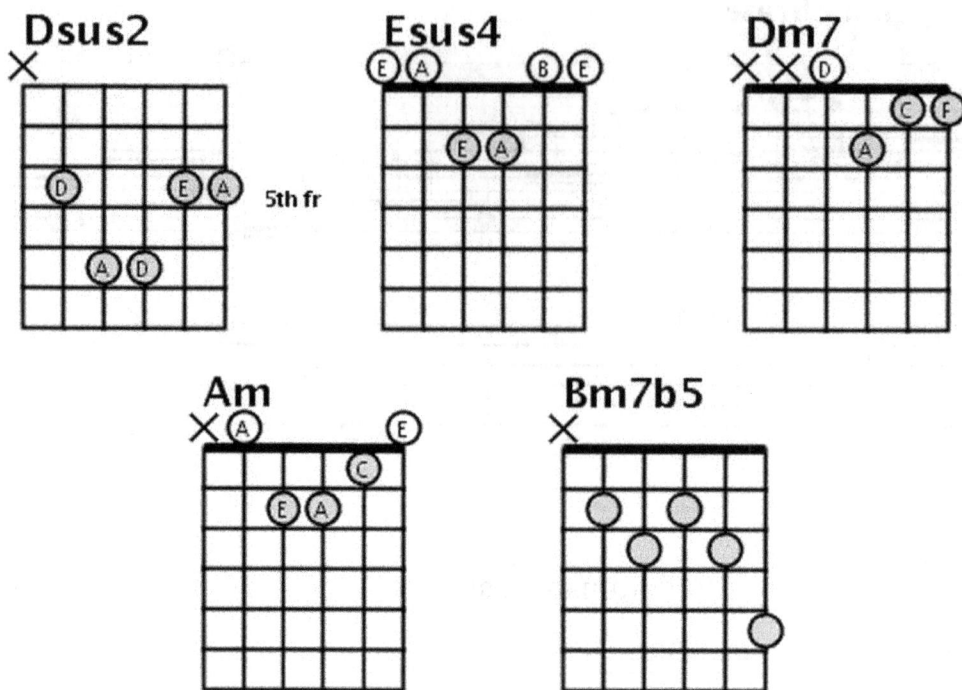

Dsus2   **Esus4**   **Dm7**

5th fr

Am   **Bm7b5**

RECAP:

♫ The harmonic minor is a natural minor (Aeolian mode) with a raised 7 (M7).

♫ The Phrygian dominant scale is the 5th mode of the harmonic minor scale.

♫ There is no harmonic minor or melodic minor key. They use the key of A natural minor (Relative minor of C).

♫ The Phrygian Dominant scale is the same as the Phrygian mode, but with a raised 3 (M3).

♫ The Phrygian dominant scale is a major scale, having a M3.

♫ The natural minor scale is the minor + Phrygian tetrachords.

♫ The harmonic minor is the minor + Gypsy (harmonic) tetrachords.

♫ The Phrygian dominant is the Gypsy + Phrygian tetrachords.

♫ The harmonic and Phrygian dominant scales' chords include two dim/m7b5, one +/maj7+5, and one m/min(maj7). This makes for mainly unusable chord progressions. It's better to plan the scales based out of 5 chords or within the normal triads (non-seventh chords) within the scales.

Chapter 3 – *Arabic and Hungarian Minor*

The Arabic and Hungarian minor scales are also called the double harmonic major and the double harmonic minor scales, respectively. In order to eliminate the confusion and reduce some typing on my part, I have elected to call these by their also known as names.

ARABIC SCALE:

The Arabic scale is called the double harmonic (major) scale because of its tetrachords structure. It contains two Gypsy, also called harmonic, tetrachords.

The Arabic scale is a Gypsy bottom and a Gypsy upper tetrachord combination.

H-WH-H   W   H-WH-H

If we put this in the format of degrees:

Arabic scale: 1-b2-3-4-5-b6-7

Intervals: P1-m2-M3-P4-P5-m6-M7

This scale is not one that is used in Western music much. I have never used it, personally. In many of the exotic scales, as previously discussed, you will either have to have the "perfect storm" situation, or specifically write a chord pattern to use these. That isn't to say that it can't happen or that you shouldn't try to use them.

Being that this is a major scale, we should look at it as it compared to the C "natural" major scale (Ionian mode).

-C major scale: **C-D-E-F-G-A-B-C**

-C Arabic scale: **C-Db-E-F-G-Ab-B-C**

Table 3-1:

C Major Triad / Seven Chord	C Arabic Triad / Seven Chord
C/Cmaj7	C/Cmaj7
Dm/Dm7	Db/Dbmaj7
Em/Em7	Em/Edim7#5
F/Fmaj7	Fm/Fm(maj7)
G/G7	Gmajb5/Gmaj7b5
Am/Am7	Ab+/Ab+maj7
Bdim/Bm7b5	B bb3 b5/B bb3(maj7)

The Edim7#5 and the B bb3(maj7) are the closest names that I could come up with using the architecture of the scale and intervals. The Edim7#5 would more commonly be called an Em6, but the 6 of the Arabic scale is a C. the B bb3(maj7) would more commonly be referred to as Db7, but I am trying to compare it to the C major scale.

Tab 3-1: C Arabic scale chords

We can see the unconventional chord spellings and odd chord architecture, based out of the Arabic scale. So as mentioned before, if you play out of the 5 chords or the I-iv-v could open up opportunities.

C Double Harmonic Major

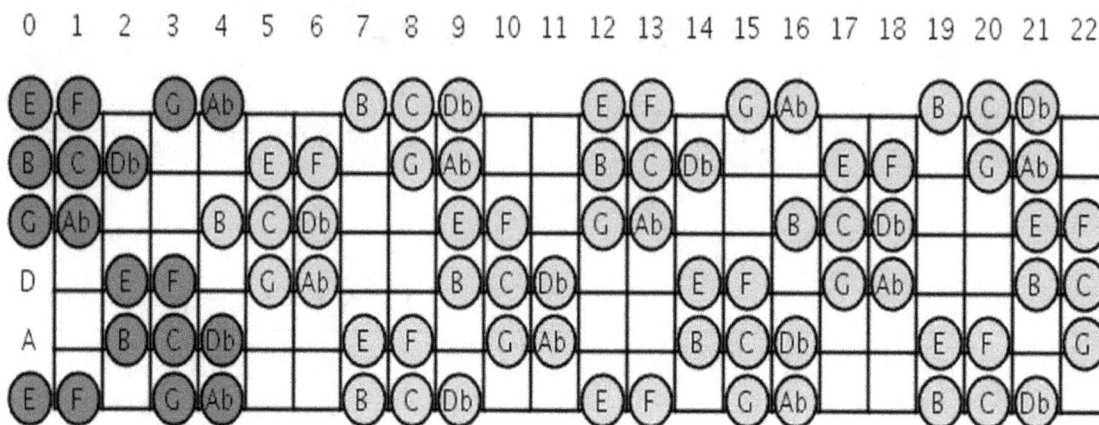

C Arabic scale / C Double Harmonic Major

List of chords to play A Arabic scale over:

C major, Db major, E major, Dbm, Em, Fm, C5, Db5, E5, F5

Fsus2, Csus4, C+, E+, Ab+

Db7, Dbm7, CM7, DbM7

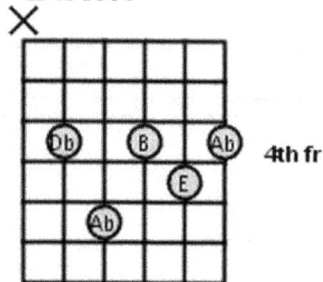

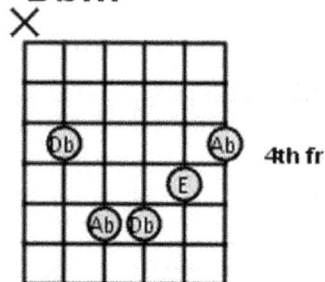

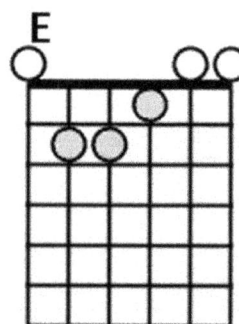

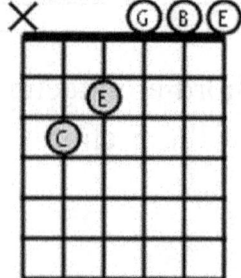

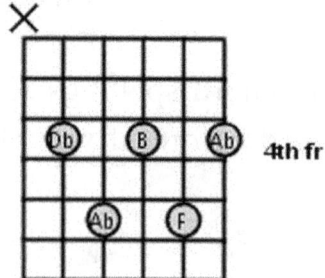

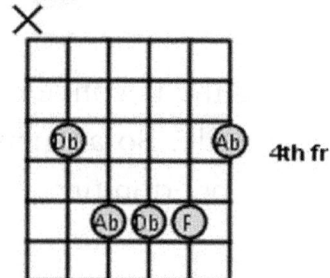

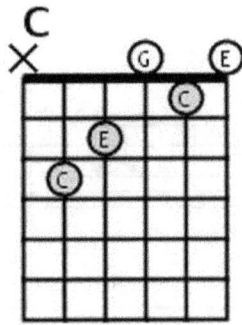

Tab 3-2: C Arabic scale

Gtr I   C   Db   E   F   G   Ab   B   C   Db   E   F   G   Ab   B   C

Tab 3-3: C Arabic scale phrase

Gtr I

Tab 3-4: C Arabic scale phrase

HUNGARIAN MINOR:

The Hungarian minor scale is also known as the double harmonic minor scale, the Hungarian Gypsy scale, Gypsy minor scale, Spanish Gypsy scale, etc. This scale is the fourth mode of the Arabic scale.

The Hungarian minor is a Nikriz maqam, a pentachord and a Gypsy upper tetrachord combination.

    W-H-WH-H   H-WH-H

Looking at the notes compared to the natural minor scale:

-Natural minor scale: **A-B-C-D-E-F-G**

-Hungarian minor scale: **A-B-C-D#-E-F-G#**

If we put this in the format of degrees:

-Natural minor: 1-2-b3-4-5-b6-b7

-Hungarian minor: 1-2-b3-#4-5-b6-7

Intervals of natural minor: P1-M2-m3-P4-P5-m6-m7

Intervals of Hungarian minor: P1-M2-m3-A4-P5-m6-M7

Table 3-2:

A Natural Minor Triad/Seven Chord	A Hungarian Minor Triad/Seven Chord
Am/Am7	Am/Am(maj7)
Bdim/Bm7b5	Bmajb5/B7b5
C major/Cmaj7	C+/Cmaj7#5
Dm/Dm7	D# bb3 b5/D# bb3 b5(maj7)
Em/Em7	E major/E7
F major/Fmaj7	F major/Fmaj7
G major/G7	G#m/G#m6 (bbb7)

The chords from the Hungarian minor have D# chords that don't exist. The chords would be deemed sus4 chords conventionally (or Eb chords). The G#m6 is really a G#m with a triple flat seven, which doesn't exist either (the max allowed is a double flat).

Tab 3-5: A Hungarian minor chords

A Hungarian Gypsy

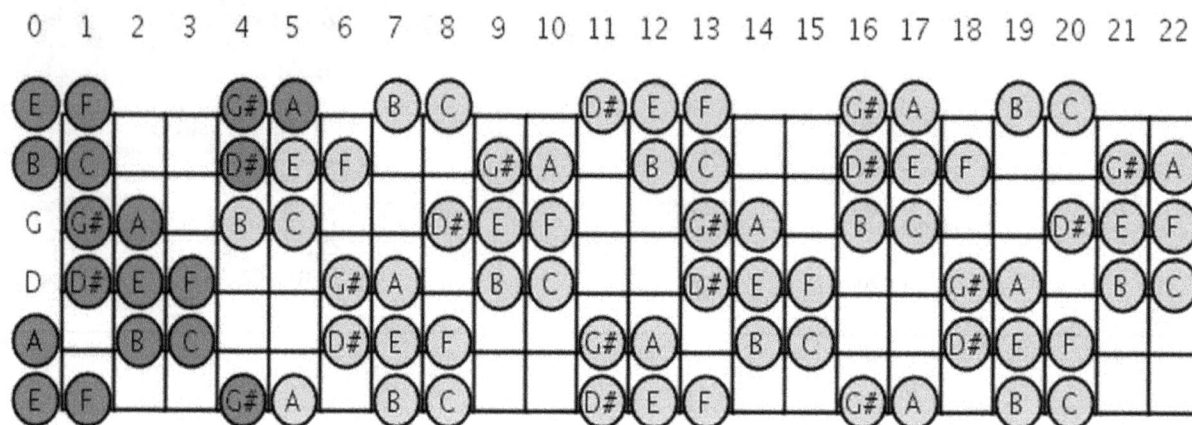

List of chords to play A Hungarian minor (Hungarian Gypsy) scale over:

E major, F major, G# major, Fm, G#m, Am, E5, F5, G#5, A5

Asus2, Esus4, C+, E+, G#+

F7, Fm7, EM7, FM7, Fm(major7), Am(major7), Fm7b5

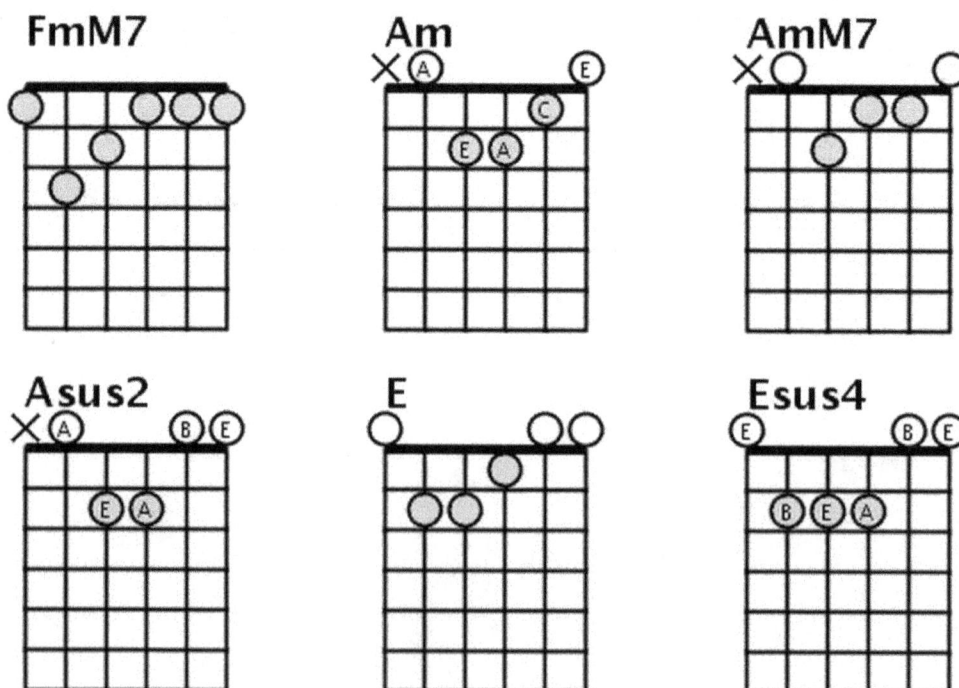

F **FM7** **Fm**

G#m **G#**

4th fr 4th fr

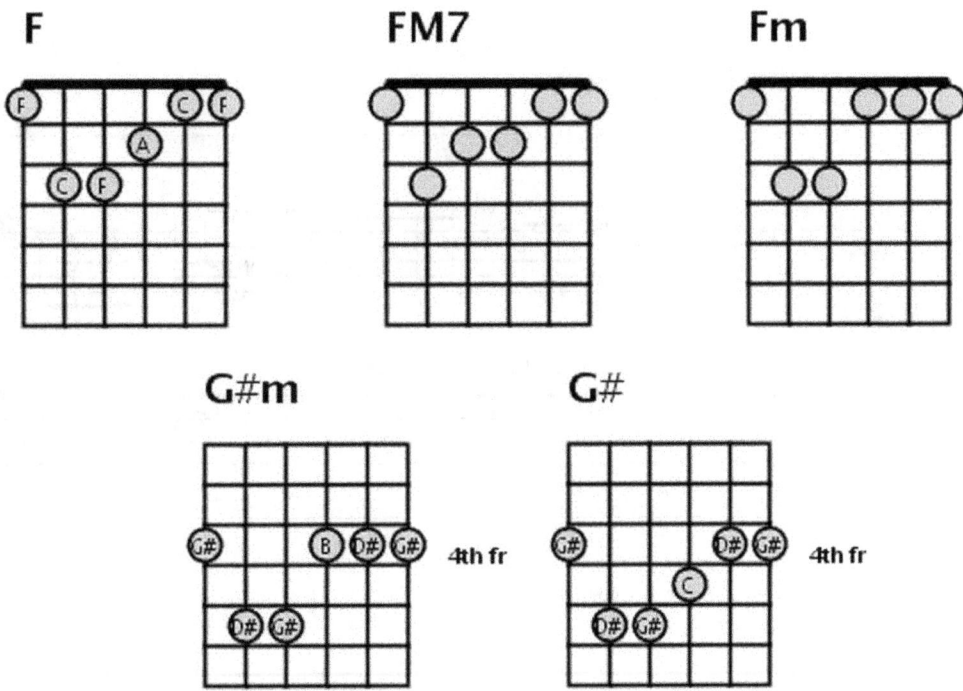

Tab 3-6: A Hungarian minor scale

Gtr I A B C D# E F G# A B C D# E F G# A

```
T                              4   5
A                  6   7   4   5   6
B   5   7   8   6  7  8
```

Tab 3-7: A Hungarian minor phrase

Gtr I

```
T                                      9   10 12 13   11 12 13   16 17
A                6   7 6 9 7  10 9  10  8   9 8 10 9  10
B   7 5 8 7  8  6  8 7 6 8 7  8
```

Tab 3-8: A Hungarian minor phrase

RECAP:

♫♪ The Arabic scale is the combination of two Gypsy tetrachords.

♫♪ The Arabic scale is a major scale.

♫♪ The seventh chords created from the Arabic scale are a bit unconventional.

♫♪ Using the Arabic scale is best when a passage is written for it.

♫♪ The Hungarian minor is the 4th mode of the Arabic scale.

♫♪ The Hungarian minor is a combination of the Nikriz maqam, a pentachord, and the Phrygian tetrachord.

♫♪ The Hungarian minor is similar to the harmonic minor, but with a raised 4th.

♫♪ Many triads and seventh chords created from the Hungarian minor are similarly strange and unconventional like those created from the Arabic scale.

♫♪ It is best to write a song specifically for these scales or to be strategic and use them over the 5 chords, which may be easier to find together within a song.

Chapter 4 – *Neapolitan Major and Neapolitan Minor*

These Neapolitan scales, both major and minor, are two exotic scales that, again, may not find much use in your guitar playing vocabulary. Just like some of the other exotic scales, finding a place for them will require either creativity or a passage written specifically for them. Another odd thing to take a note of is that both the Neapolitan major **and** the Neapolitan minor are *minor* scales.

NEAPOLITAN MAJOR

The Neapolitan major, interestingly, is the same as an ascending melodic minor, but it has a flattened 2nd (m2).

The Neapolitan major is a Phrygian bottom and a minor upper tetrachord combination.

H-W-W   W   W-W-H

Looking at the notes compared to the natural minor scale:

-Natural minor scale: **A-B-C-D-E-F-G**

-Neapolitan major scale: **A-Bb-C-D-E-F#-G#**

If we put this in the format of degrees:

-Natural minor: 1-2-b3-4-5-b6-b7

-Neapolitan major: 1-b2-b3-4-5-6-7

Intervals of natural minor: P1-M2-m3-P4-P5-m6-m7

Intervals of Neapolitan major: P1-m2-m3-P4-P5-M6-M7

Table 4-1:

A Natural Minor Triad/Seven Chord	A Neapolitan Major Triad/Seven Chord
Am/Am7	Am/Am(maj7)
Bdim/Bm7b5	Bb+/Bb+maj7
C major/Cmaj7	C+/C+7
Dm/Dm7	D major/D7
Em/Em7	E major b5/E7b5
F major/Fmaj7	F#dim/F#m7b5
G major/G7	G#bb3 b5/G#bb3 b7b5

The chords created by the Neapolitan major yields a minor for a 1 chord, which defeats the concept of being a major scale. There are two augmented chords, three dominant seven chords (one of which has a double flat 3rd), and a minor(maj7) chord.

Tab 4-1: A Neapolitan major chords

A Neapolitan Major

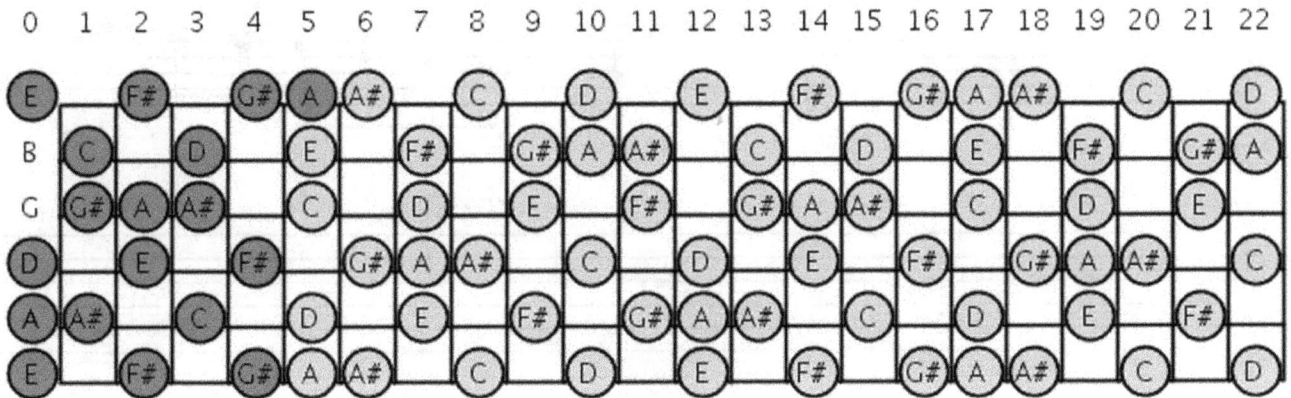

List of chords to play A Neapolitan major scale over:

D major, Am, D5, A5

Dsus2, Asus4, E b5, C+, D+, E+, Gb+, Ab+, Bb+

Gbm7b5, D7

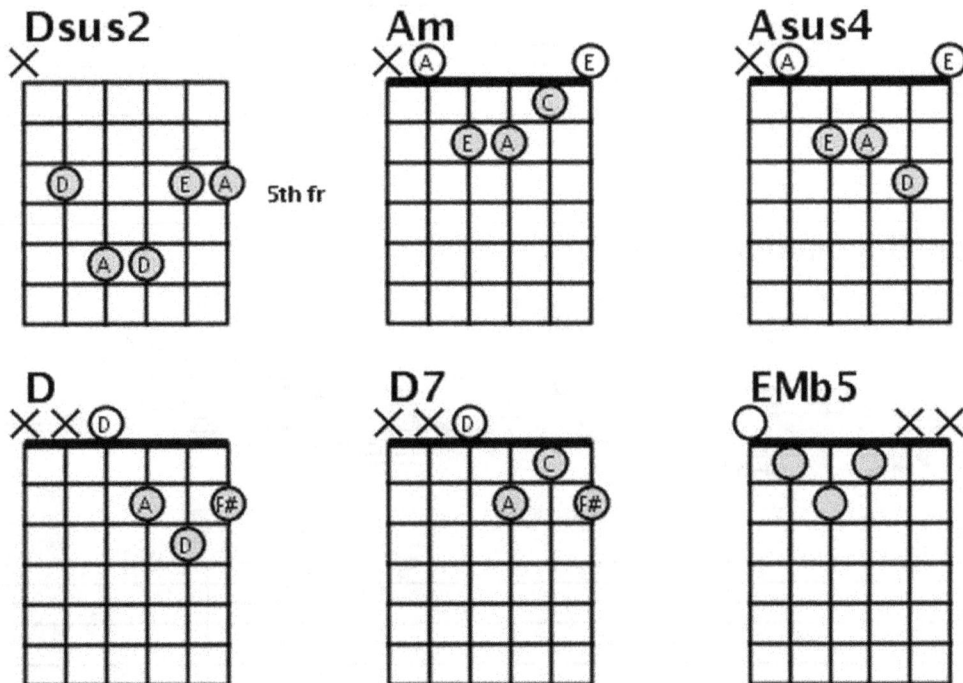

Tab 4-2: A Neapolitan major scale

```
Gtr I  A  Bb  C  D  E  F#  G#  A      Bb  C  D  E  F#  G#  A

T                                                    5   7   9
A                              4   6   7      3   5   7           5
B        5  6   3   5   7
```

Tab 4-3: A Neapolitan major scale

```
Gtr I  A  Bb  C  D  E  F#  G#  A   Bb  C  D  E  F#  G#  A  Bb   C  D  E  F#  G#  A
                                                                8  10  12  14  16  17
T                                              7   9  10  11
A                          6   7      8   5   7   9
B        5   6   8   5   7   9
                                                            sl.  sl.           sl.
```

Tab 4-4: A Neapolitan major phrase

```
Gtr I

T                                                    8   10 12 14        12 17
A                                         5   7   9        13 11 10 13
B    5 4 5 6   6 5 4 5 6   4 5 6   3 5   7 9   9 7 5  6 7 8  7 9 10
         3                                 6
                                sl.                      sl.        sl.
```

Tab 4-5: A Neapolitan major phrase

NEAPOLITAN MINOR

The Neapolitan minor is the same as the Phrygian mode, but with a raised seventh (M7).

The Neapolitan minor is a Phrygian bottom and a Gypsy upper tetrachord combination.

H-W-W   W   H-WH-H

Looking at the notes compared to the natural minor scale:

-Natural minor scale: **A-B-C-D-E-F-G**

-Neapolitan minor scale: **A-Bb-C-D-E-F-G#**

If we put this in the format of degrees:

-Natural minor: 1-2-b3-4-5-b6-b7

-Neapolitan minor: 1-b2-b3-4-5-b6-7

Intervals of natural minor: P1-M2-m3-P4-P5-m6-m7

Intervals of Neapolitan major: P1-m2-m3-P4-P5-m6-M7

Table 4-2:

A Natural Minor Triad/Seven Chord	A Neapolitan Minor Triad/Seven Chord
Am/Am7	Am/Am(maj7)
Bdim/Bm7b5	Bb major/Bbmaj7
C major/Cm7	C+/C+7
Dm/Dm7	Dm/Dm7
Em/Em7	E major b5/E7b5
F major/Fmaj7	F major/Fmaj7
G major/G7	G#bb3 b5/G#bb3 bb7 b5

The chords created by the Neapolitan minor yields a minor(maj7), one augmented chord, three dominant seven chords, and one really messed up chord.

Tab 4-6: A Neapolitan minor chords

A Neapolitan Minor

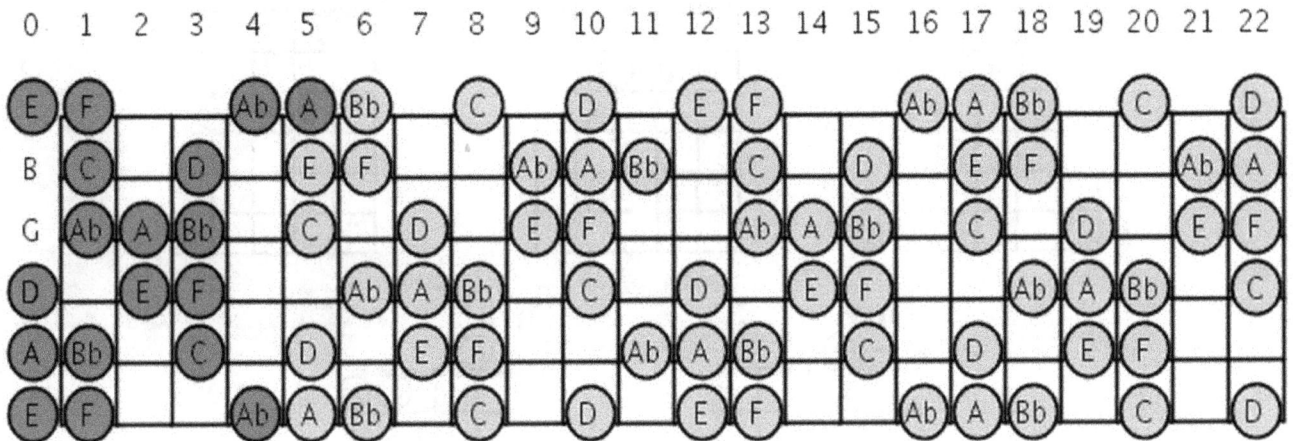

List of chords to play A Neapolitan minor scale over:

F major, Bb major, Dm, Fm, Am, D5, F5, A5, Bb5

Dsus2, Bbsus2, Fsus4, Asus4, C+, E+, Ab+,

Bb7, Dm7, FM7, BbM7, Dm7b5

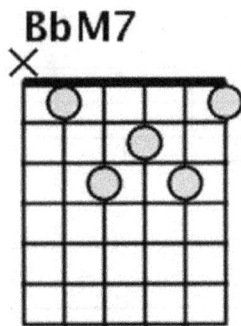

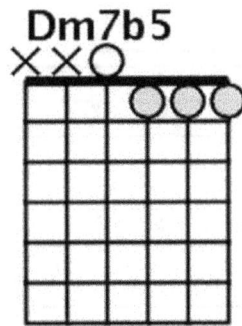

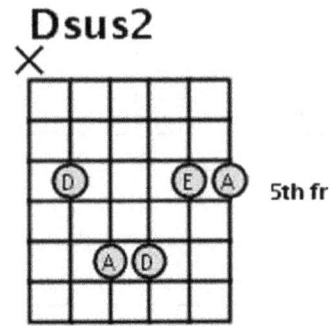

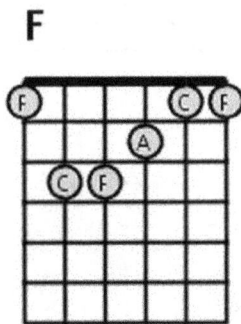

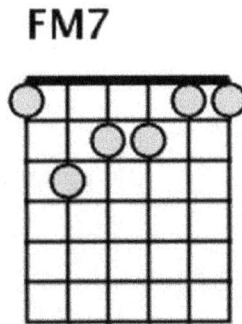

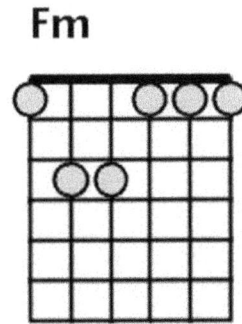

Am

Asus4

Bb

Dm

Dm7

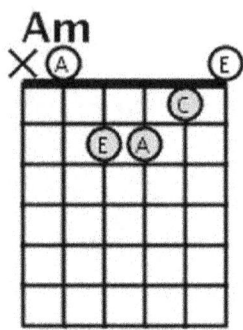

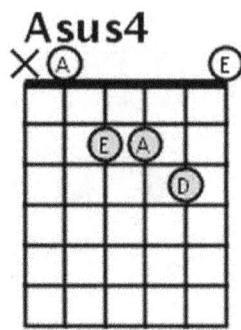

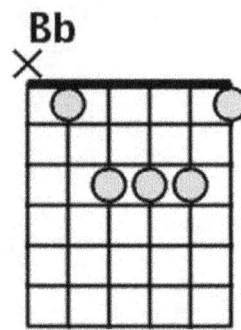

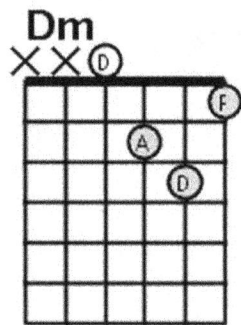

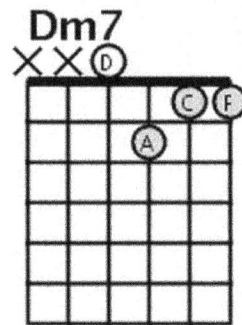

Tab 4-7: A Neapolitan minor scale

| Gtr I | A | Bb | C | D | E | F | G# | A | | Bb | C | D | E | F | G# | A |

Tab 4-8: A Neapolitan minor phrase

Tab 4-9: A Neapolitan minor phrase

RECAP:

♫ The Neapolitan major scale is the combination of a Phrygian bottom and minor upper tetrachords.

♫ The Neapolitan major scale is a minor scale.

♫ The Neapolitan major is the same as an ascending melodic minor, but it has a m2.

♫ The Neapolitan minor scale is the combination of a Phrygian bottom and Gypsy upper tetrachords.

♫ The Neapolitan minor is the same as the Phrygian mode, but with a M7.

♫ Both Neapolitan scales yield some pretty useless seventh chords.

Chapter 5 – *Hirajoshi & Its Modes*

These Japanese scales are pentatonic. The most common mode is the Iwato, which is the second mode of the Hirajoshi scale. The Hirajoshi is a minor scale, but the Iwato is neither; it skips the third interval.

HIRAJOSHI SCALE

The Hirajoshi scale is a pentatonic scale.

Looking at the notes compared to the natural minor scale:

-Natural minor scale: **A-B-C-D-E-F-G**

-Hirajoshi scale: **A-B-C-E-F**

If we put this in the format of degrees:

-Natural minor: 1-2-b3-4-5-b6-b7

-Hirajoshi scale: 1-2-b3-5-b6

Intervals of natural minor: P1-M2-m3-P4-P5-m6-m7

Intervals of Hirajoshi scale: P1-M2-m3-P5-m6

Table 5-1:

A Natural Minor Triad/Seven Chord	A Hirajoshi Triad/Seven Chord
Am/Am7	Am/Am7
Bdim/Bm7b5	B5/Bbmaj7 no 3rd
C major/Cm7	C no 5/Cmaj7 no 5
Dm/Dm7	No D Interval
Em/Em7	E no 5
F major/Fmaj7	F major/Fmaj7
G major/G7	No G Interval

The chords of the Hirajoshi scale allow for flexibility, giving the opportunity to play over many chords. Being that there are no 4th or 7th intervals, as long as you don't play some dissonant interval, there should be an allowance for freedom.

Tab 5-1: A Hirajoshi chords

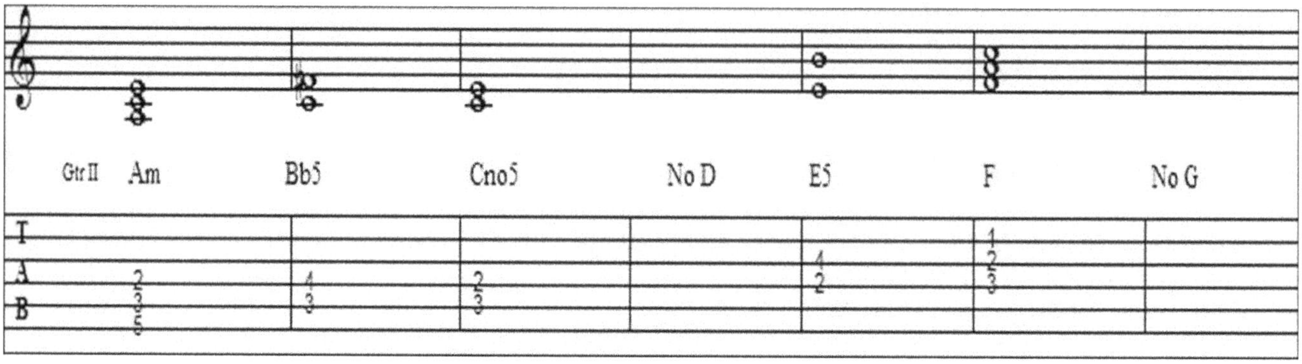

A Hirajoshi Scale

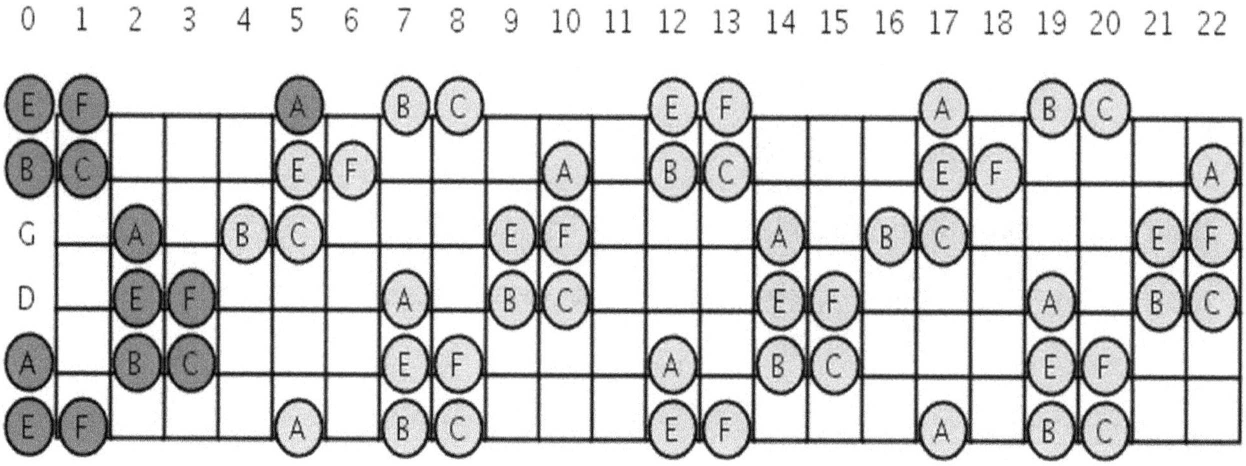

List of chords to play A Hirajoshi scale over:

F major, Am, E5, F5, A5

Asus2, Esus4, FM7

F   **Am**   **Am**

5th fr

Asus2   **Esus4**   **Esus4**

F5

Tab 5-2: A Hirajoshi scale

Gtr I   A   B   C   E   F   A   B   C   E   F   A   B   C   E   F   A

Tab 5-3: A Hirajoshi phrase

IWATO SCALE

The Iwato scale is a pentatonic scale. It is the second mode of the Hirajoshi scale. It gets its own heading because it is the most used of the Hirojoshi modes. The Iwato scale has no 3rd interval, which means that it has no major or minor characteristic. The issue that you run into though is the Eb. This means that the 5th interval is flattened. Let's get this scale laid out and look at its chords and intervals in more depth.

Looking at the notes compared to the natural minor scale:

-Natural minor scale: **A-B-C-D-E-F-G**

-Iwato scale: **A-Bb-D-Eb-G**

If we put this in the format of degrees:

-Natural major: 1-2-3-4-5-6-7

-Iwato scale: 1-b2-4-b5-b7

Intervals of natural minor: P1-M2-m3-P4-P5-m6-m7

Intervals of Iwato scale: P1-m2-P4-d5-m7

Table 5-2:

A Natural Minor Triad/Seven Chord	A Iwato Triad/Seven Chord
Am/Am7	A no 3rd/A7no 3rd
Bdim/Bm7b5	Bb major no 5/Bbmaj7 no 5
C major/Cmaj7	No C Interval
Dm/Dm7	D no 3rd
Em/Em7	Eb major/Ebmaj7
F major/Fmaj7	No F Interval
G major/G7	Gm/Gm7

The notes of the A Iwato scale are within the A Locrian mode:

-A Locrian: **A-Bb-C-D-Eb-F-G**

-A Iwato: **A-Bb-D-Eb-G**

A simpler way to look at it would be to use the A Iwato over the key of Bb major:

-Bb major: **Bb-C-D-Eb-F-G-A**

-A Iwato: **A-Bb-D-Eb-G**

The A Locrian mode is the seventh mode in the key of Bb major. So, any major key that you play in, if you go to the major seventh (one semitone behind the root), you can play that Iwato scale over it, e.g., if you're playing in the key of G major, play the F# Iwato scale over it.

This is my trick to using modes and scales over keys. In essence you are playing the Iwato, but theoretically, you are playing the 2nd mode of the Hirajoshi scale (The mode starting on G, not F#), but you don't have to memorize each mode and how to play each one, you only need to learn one form and how to use it.

Tab 5-4: A Iwato chords

Gtr II	A b5	Bb no5	No C	D5	Eb	No F	Gm

A Iwato

List of chords to play A Hirajoshi scale over:

Eb major, Gm, D5, Eb5, G5

Gsus2, Dsus4,

Eb major b5, Gm #5, EbM7

Chord diagrams: Gsus2, Dsus4, Gm, EbM7 (6th fr), Eb (6th fr)

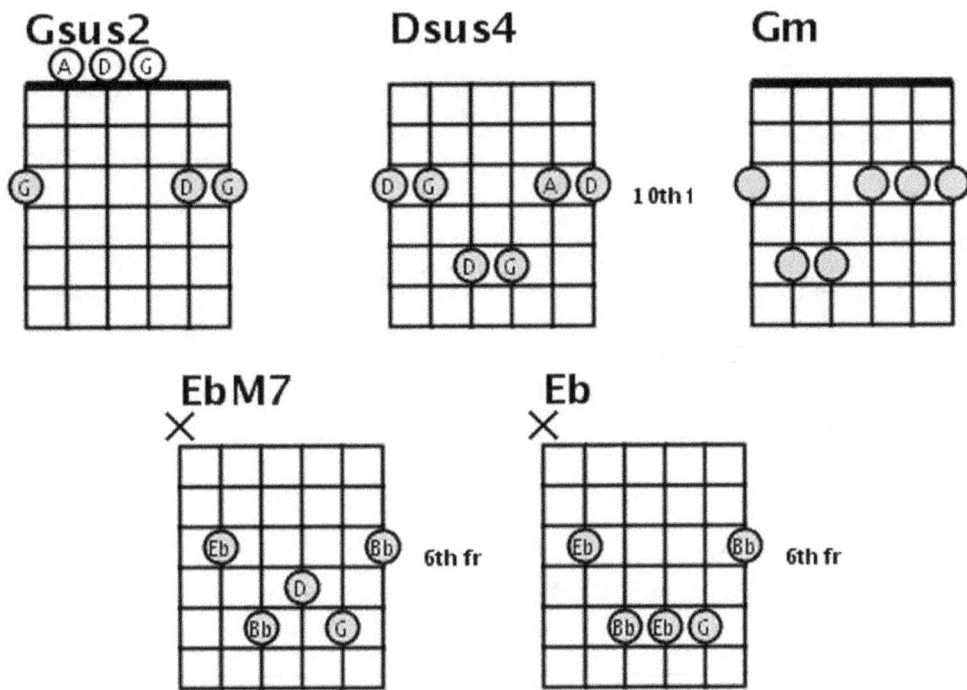

Tab 5-5: A Iwato scale

Tab 5-6: A Iwato phrase

HIRAJOSHI MODES

Below I will lay out the steps and notes, of the modes, in comparison to each other within the Hirojoshi scale.

Looking at the notes of the Hirojoshi modes:

-Hirojoshi scale: **A-B-C-E-F**

-Iwato scale: **A-Bb-D-Eb-G**

-Kumoi: **A-C#-D-F#-G#**

-Hon Kumoi Shiouzhi: **A-Bb-D-E-F**

- Chinese scale: **A-C#-D#-E-G#**

Let's look at the steps:

-Hirojoshi scale: W-H-WW-H-WW

-Iwato scale: H-WW-H-WW-W

-Kumoi: WW-H-WW-W-H

-Hon Kumoi Shiouzhi: H-WW-W-H-WW

- Chinese scale: WW-W-H-WW-H

If we put this in the format of degrees:

-Hirojoshi scale: 1-2-b3-5-b6

-Iwato scale: 1-b2-4-b5-b7

-Kumoi: 1-3-4-6-7

-Hon Kumoi Shiouzhi: 1-b2-4-5-b6

-Chinese scale: 1-3-#4-5-7

Looking at the notes of the Hirojoshi modes as they compare to major scale modes:

Table 5-3:

Scale/Mode	Notes
A Hirajoshi Scale	A-B-C-E-F
A Aeolian Mode	A-B-C-D-E-F-G
A Iwato Scale	A-Bb-D-Eb-G
A Locrian Mode	A-Bb-C-D-Eb-F-G
A Kumoi Scale	A-C#-D-F#-G#
A Ionian Mode	A-B-C#-D-E-F#-G#
A Hon Kumoi Shiouzhi Scale	A-Bb-D-E-F
A Phrygian Mode	A-Bb-C-D-E-F-G
A Chinese Scale	A-C#-D#-E-G#
A Lydian Mode	A-B-C#-D#-E-F#-G#

The modes of the Hirajoshi scale are all similar to modes of the major scale. This shouldn't be too big of a surprise since the A Hirojoshi looks so much like the A natural minor scale. The following neck diagrams will look like the same thing just moved a little. This is because they are just modes of the same scale. The only thing that is happening it the root note is starting on a different interval, but you know this already because you read one of my other books, right? Well, I won't get my hopes up. Let's continue…

A Hirajoshi Scale

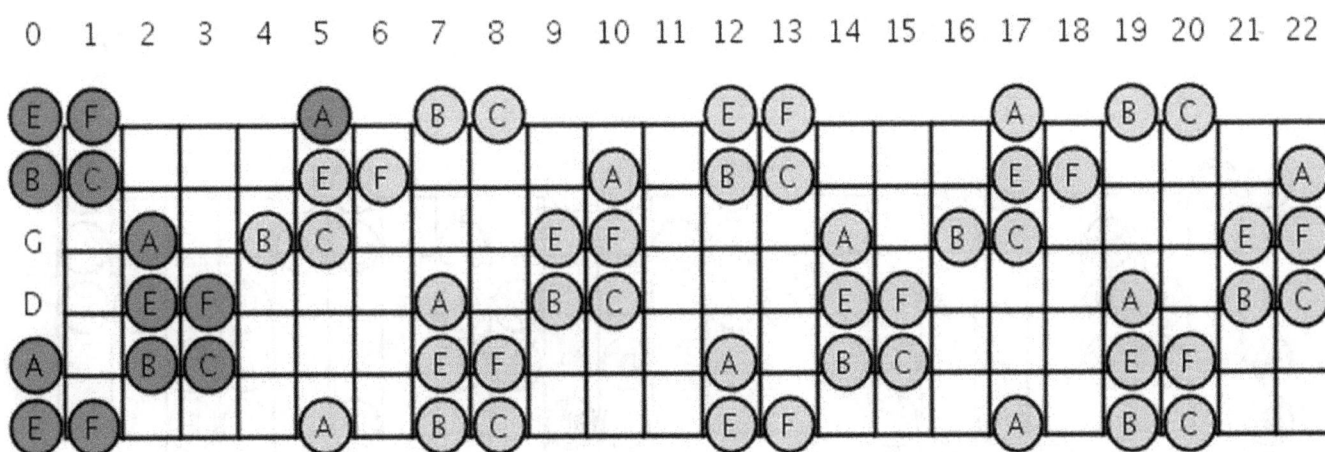

A Iwato

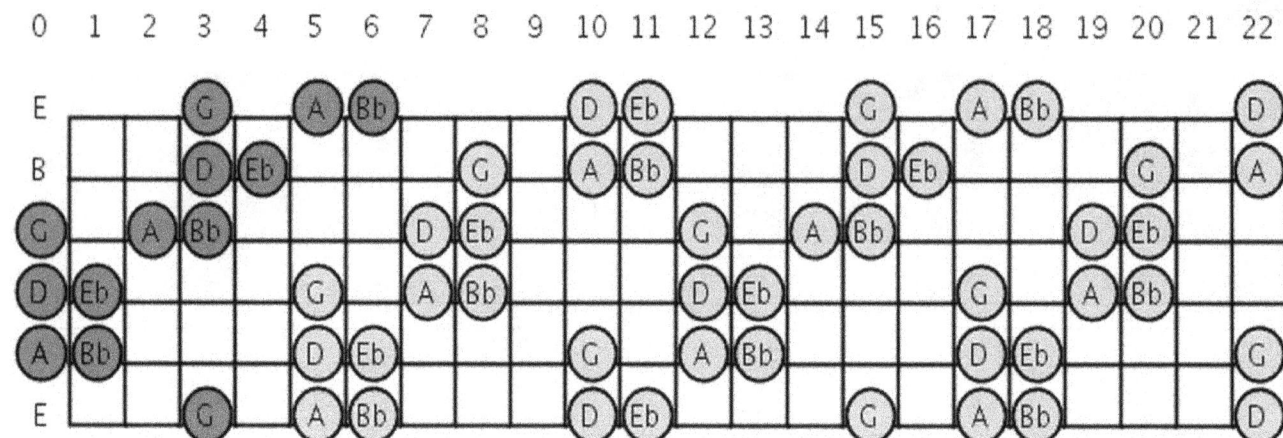

A Kumoi Scale

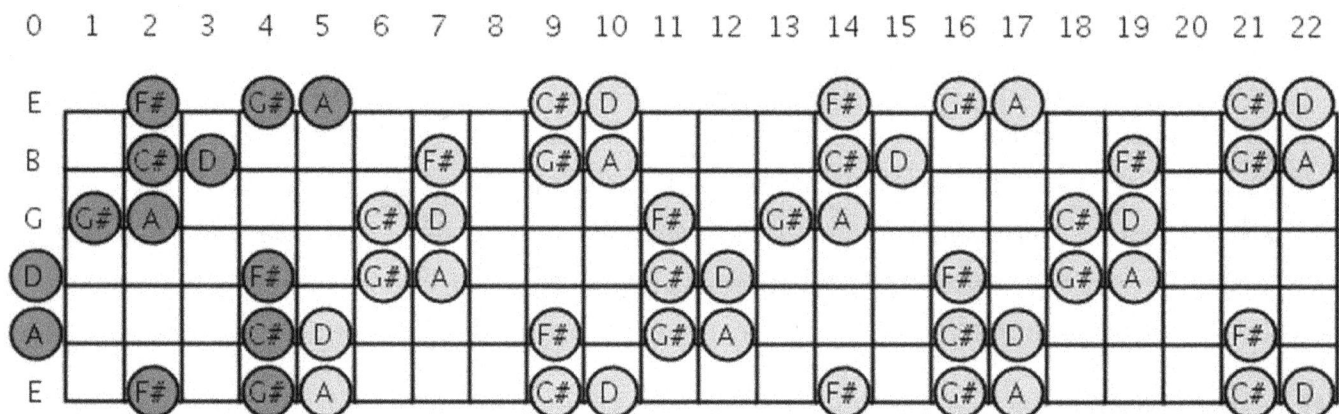

A Hon Kumoi Shiouzhi scale

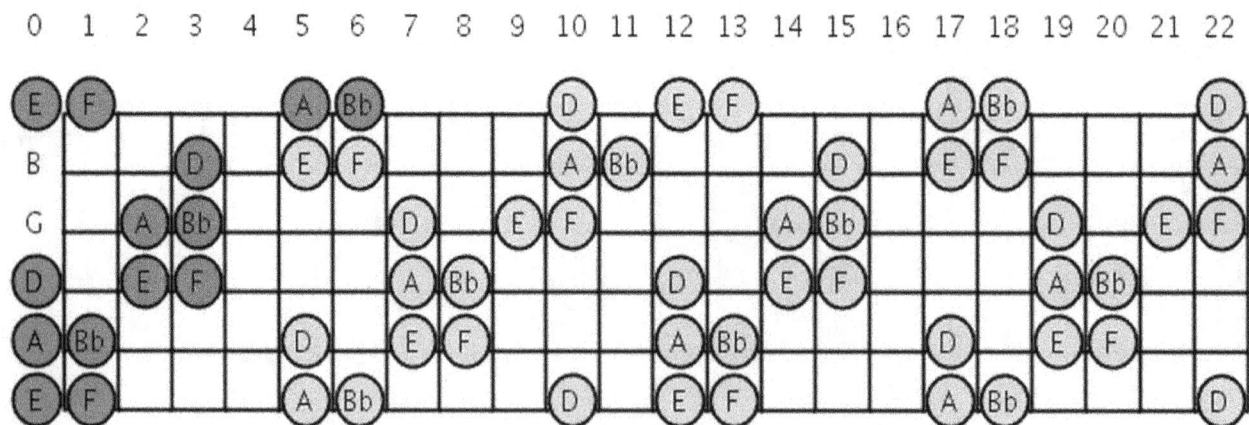

A Chinese Scale

Tab 5-7: A Hirojoshi modes

GtrI A Hirajoshi   A Iwato   A Kumoi   A Hon Kumoi Shiouzhi   A Chinese Scale

RECAP:

♫ The Hirajoshi scale is a Japanese pentatonic scale.

♫ The Hirajoshi scale is a major scale.

♫ The Iwato scale is the most used mode of the Hirajoshi scale.

♫ The Iwato scale is the second mode of the Hirajoshi scale.

♫ The Iwato scale is neither major nor minor, because it doesn't have a 3rd interval.

♫ All of the Hirajoshi modes are directly comparable to modes of the major scale.

♫ The Hirajoshi modes seem to have the most normal cords.

♫ The modes of the Hirajoshi seem to sound very good and can be used in the place of the modes to get an Asian sound.

Chapter 6 – *Yo, In Sen, & Oriental Scales*

The Yo and the In Sen are traditional Japanese scales. These two scales can be heard in traditional gagaku and koto music. The Oriental scale is the 5th mode of the Arabic scale.

YO SCALE:

The Yo scale is thought to as having a bright sound.

The Yo scale is a pentatonic scale with the following step progression:

W-WH-W-W-WH

If we put this in the format of degrees:

Yo scale: 1-2-4-5-6

Intervals: P1-M2-P4-P5-M6

Being that this scale has no 3rd, we will look at it as it compared to the C "natural" major scale (Ionian mode).

-C major scale: **C-D-E-F-G-A-B**

-C Yo scale: **C-D-F-G-A**

Table 6-1:

C Major Triad/Seven Chord	C Yo Triad/Seven Chord
C major/Cm7	C5
Dm/Dm7	Dm/Dm7
Em/Em7	No E Interval
F major/Fmaj7	F major
G major/G7	G5
Am/Am7	Am no 5/Am7 no 5
Bdim/Bm7b5	No B Interval

If you think about it, the Yo scale has a lot of similar chords that are in the C major scale/A Aeolian. This could be squeezed into many songs with chords derived from the major scale. This scale could have plenty of applications.

Tab 6-1: A Yo scale chords

C Yo

List of chords to play C Yo scale over:

F major, Dm, C5, D5, F5, G5

Csus2, Fsus2, Gsus2, Csus4, Dsus4, Gsus4

Dm7

Gsus4 **Csus2** **Csus4** 8th fr

Dm **Dm7** **Dsus2** 5th fr

Dsus4 10th fr **F** **Gsus2**

Tab 6-2: A Yo scale

Gtr I   A C D F G A C D   F G A   A C D F G A C D   F G A

Tab 6-3: A Yo scale phrase

Tab 6-4: A Yo scale phrase

IN SEN SCALE:

The In Sen scale has the same notes as seen in the Phrygian scale.

The In Sen scale is a pentatonic scale with the following step progression:

H-WW-W-WH-W

If we put this in the format of degrees:

In Sen scale: 1-b2-4-5-b7

Intervals: P1-m2-P4-P5-m7

Being that this scale is similar to the Phrygian mode, we will look at it as it compared to the C Phrygian mode.

-C Phrygian scale: **C-Db-Eb-F-G-Ab-Bb-C**

-C In Sen scale: **C-Db-F-G-Bb**

Table 6-2:

C Phrygian Triad/Seven Chord	C In Sen Triad/Seven Chord
Cm/Cm7	C5
Db major/Dbmaj7	Db5
Eb major/Eb7	No E Interval
Fm/Fm7	F5
Gdim/Gm7b5	Gdim/Gm7b5
Ab major/Abmaj7	No A Interval
Bbm/Bbm7	Bbm

The In Sen scale has a lot of similarities to the Phrygian mode. This could be squeezed into many songs with power chords in the place of major or minor chords. This scale could have plenty of applications where a Phrygian is used.

Tab 6-5: C In Sen chords

C Traditional Japanese "in sen"

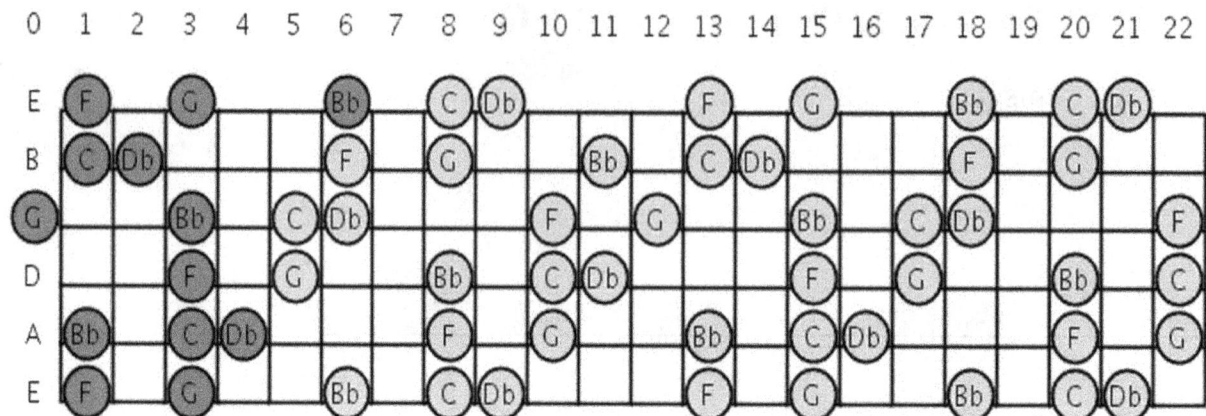

List of chords to play C In Sen scale over:

Bbm, C5, F5, Bb5

Fsus2, Bbsus2, Csus4, Fsus4

Gm7b5

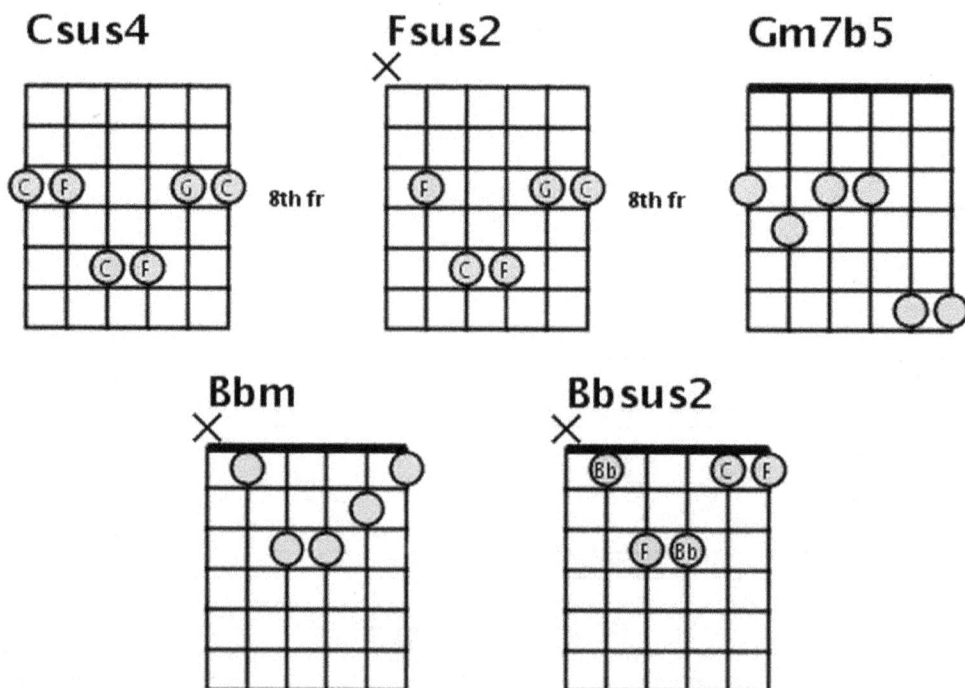

Tab 6-6: C In Sen scale

Tab 6-7: In Sen scale phrase

ORIENTAL SCALE:

The Oriental scale is the 5th mode of the Arabic scale.

The Oriental scale is a Gypsy bottom and a Lydian #2 upper tetrachord combination.

H-WH-H   H   WH-H-W

If we put this in the format of degrees:

Oriental scale: 1-b2-3-4-b5-6-b7

Intervals: P1-m2-M3-P4-d5-M6-m7

Being that this scale is a major scale, we will look at it as it compared to the C "natural" major scale (Ionian mode).

-C major scale: **C-D-E-F-G-A-B**

-C Oriental scale: **C-Db-E-F-Gb-A-Bb**

Table 6-3:

C major Triad / Seven Chord	C Oriental Triad / Seven Chord
C major/Cmaj7	Cb5/C7b5
Dm/Dm7	Db+/Db+maj7
Em/Em7	Esus2b5
F major/Fmaj7	F major/F maj7
G major/G7	Gb major/Gb maj7
Am/Am7	Am/Ambb7
Bdim/Bm7b5	Bbm/Bbm(maj7)

The Oriental scale has some interesting chords to go with it. There are a few b5 chords and an augmented, but other than that, if you like playing four power chords that are right by each other, this might be up your alley. Play around with it and see.

Tab 6-8: C Oriental Chords

GtrⅡ   C b5   Db+   Esusb5   F   Gbmaj   Am   Bbm

C Oriental

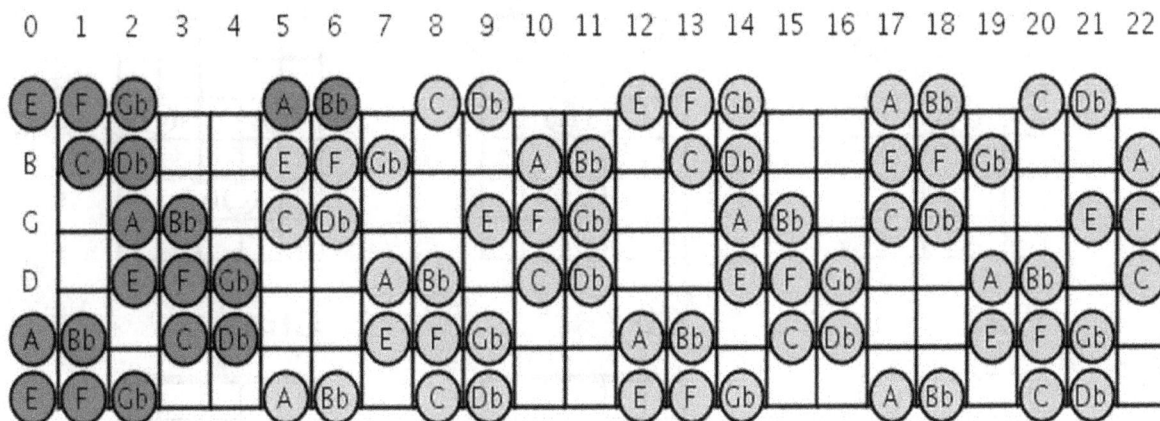

List of chords to play C Oriental scale over:

F major, Gb major, A major, Gbm, Am, Bbm, F5, Gb5, A5, Bb5

Bbsus2, Fsus4,

Gb7, Gbm7, FM7, GbM7, Gbm7b5, GbM7b5

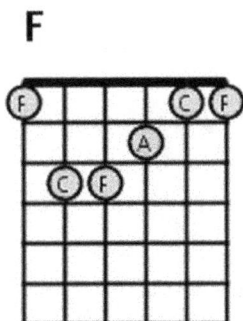

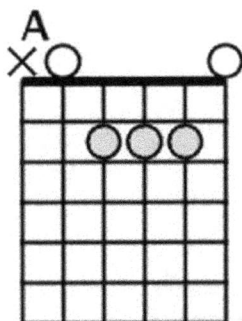

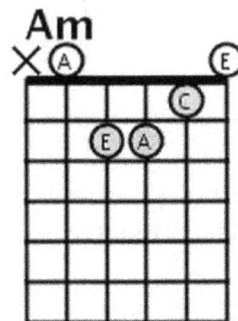

Bbm

Bbsus2

Fsus2

8th fr

FM7

Gb7

Gbm

Gb

Gbm7b5

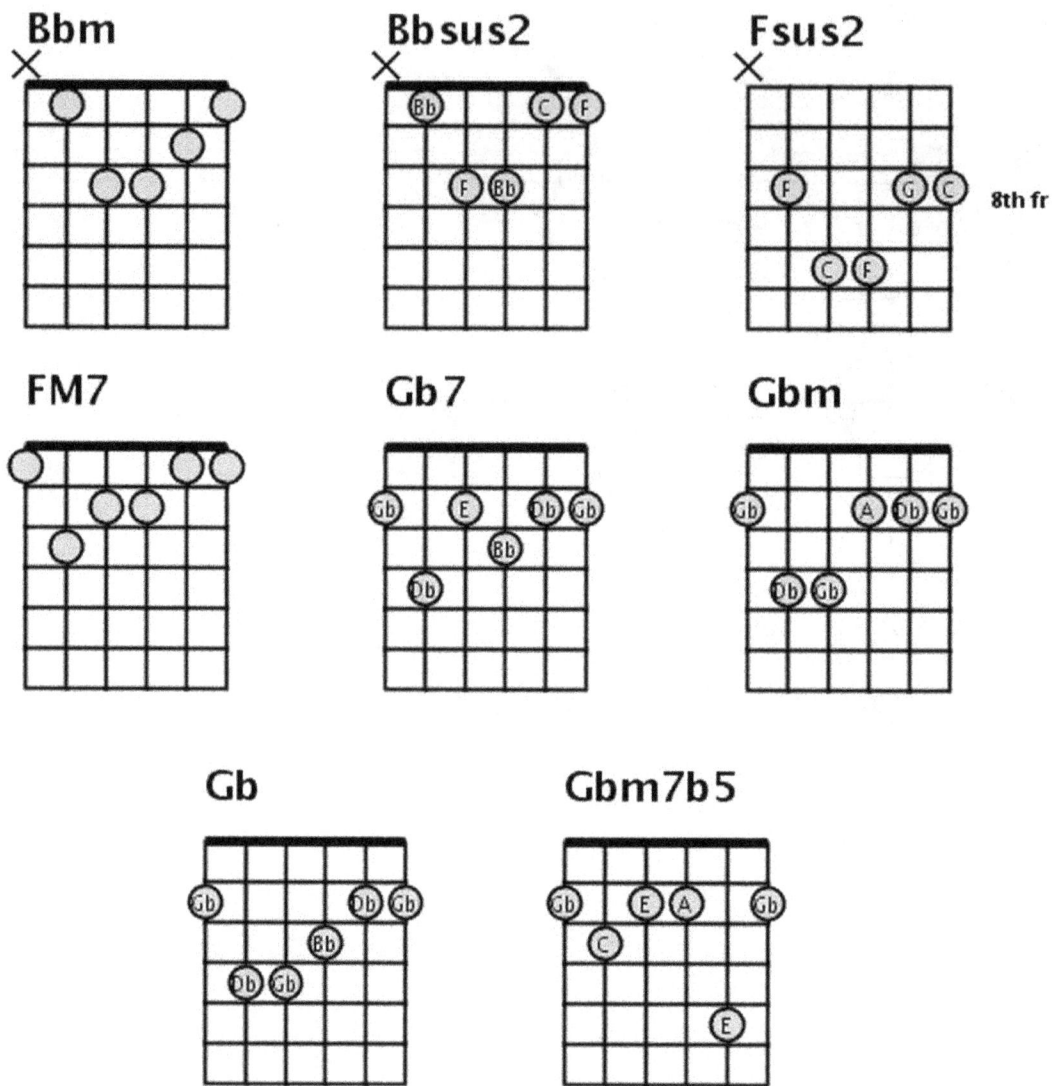

Tab 6-9: C Oriental scale

| Gtr I | C | Db | E | F | Gb | A | Bb | C | | Db | E | F | Gb | A | Bb | C |

Tab 6-10: C Oriental scale phrase

RECAP:

♫ The Yo and the In Sen are traditional Japanese scales.

♫ The Yo and In Sen are both pentatonic scales.

♫ The Oriental scale is the 5th mode of the Arabic scale.

♫ The Yo scale is neither major nor minor, because it doesn't have a 3rd interval.

♫ The Yo scale has a lot of similar chords that are in the C major scale/A Aeolian.

♫ The In Sen scale has the same notes as seen in the Phrygian scale

♫ The Oriental scale is a Gypsy bottom and a Lydian #2 upper tetrachord combination

♫ The Oriental scale is a major scale.

Some of the scales that we have covered may take some time to figure out where to use them, or you could have used a few of them already in something that you have been writing. The main thing is to try to write a passage where you could use it and see what you think about it. Some may be unusable to you, whether it is because you can't find a use for it or you think it sounds bad.

The reason this book was purchased was probably to open some new door to music, to glean some insight into more musical possibilities, or you thought the pages were layered with pixie dust and that by reading a page here and there you'd be the next Steve Vai.

I hate to break it to you, but the last sentence just isn't going to happen. You are going to have to work for it, and I hope you do become the next Steve Vai. The next section will be on arpeggios. Take consideration on what you are trying to accomplish and be vigilant and determined. I hope after the next section you become the next Paganini.

Chapter 7 – Arpeggio Introduction

The arpeggio has been around for a long time. Many newer guitarists have been incorporating them since the introduction of neoclassical guitar style, in the '80s. There are many different guitarists that are great in their own right and use the arpeggio in many different ways. The term arpeggio actually means "a harping". I bet you didn't expect that, did you?

The term arpeggio is also used to mean "broken chord". This brokenness is the succession of the notes in a chord rather than the strumming of the notes in a chord. Many pianists, such as J.S. Bach, Beethoven, and Mozart used arpeggios in their compositions. The term neoclassical guitar is a misnomer. The periods in which the main idea for the guitar, where the arpeggio was reintroduced to the world, comes from are the Baroque, Classical, and Romantic periods.

Neoclassicism is an era in itself (between the two World Wars), where musicians were using ideas based out of the prior periods that I mentioned. I guess that is why they decided to call it that for guitar. Oh well, this isn't a music history class.

The arpeggio can be used as a major part of a solo, song, or idea; or it can be used as an embellishment. The following section of this book will look at arpeggios, their construction, and some ways to play them. None of my books, up to this point, have been books on "licks". The main thing this book will focus on is the theory and construction of arpeggios.

These arpeggios have been the growing trend in music because of the sweep. A sweep is an arpeggio that is played fast and the guitarist picks down or up the strings in a sweeping motion. This raking is where the chord isn't strummed where all note tones are heard at the same time, but the notes are played one-by-one in a chord shape like usual, but the notes are sustained to hold out like a chord. There is an interesting marking to signify this type of arpeggiation. Notice how Example 1 shows arpeggiation, but the notation above it doesn't. The true notation version is Example 2 in Diagram 7-1.

Diagram 7-1:

Example 1

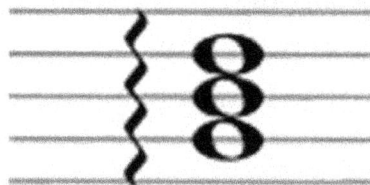

Example 2

The form of arpeggiating that is most prevalent these days consists of individual notes of a chord played successively. The usual method uses a triad and plays the notes concurrently, not out of order. This is normally in the form 1-3-5. Arpeggios can be major, minor, diminished, augmented, seventh, or whatever.

If you don't understand major scale theory or chord theory, this section will start to get confusing. Get either *A Guitarist's Guide to Theory* or *Interval and Major Scale Theory*, both of my books that explain major scale theory in detail. Sorry about all of the selfless promoting, but you need to know the basics.

Major triads consist of a 1-3-5 from the major scale. In the key of *C* this would be *C-E-G*. If we played this as an arpeggio it could have different shapes because a *C* major chord can be played as a chord many different ways. The most widely used shapes or forms are the *A*, *D*, and *E* shape.

The *A* shape comes directly from the *A* major barre chord, nothing confusing about this.

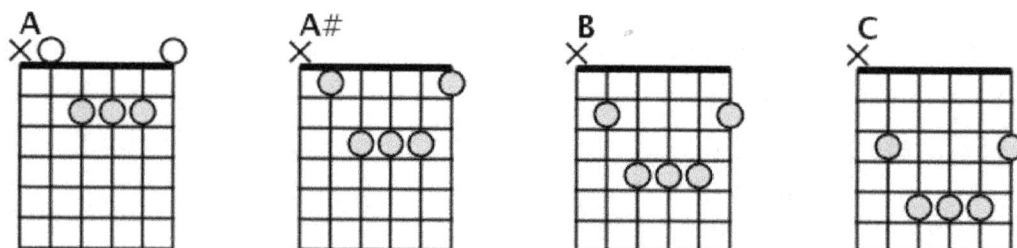

The problem with a regular *A* shaped chord is that it doesn't go in the form 1-3-5. It follows a 1-5-1-3-5 pattern, if we play the chord one note at a time. Therefore, we need to add in a 3 after the 1 and before the 5 to make this follow the desired pattern. All of the following chord shapes will be adjusted to meet the criteria of 1-3-5.

Tab 7-1:

TAB 7-1 illustrates the basic *A* shaped arpeggio. The arpeggio is a *C* major. The shape is *A* major, because it looks like the open *A* major chord. The stretch on this is quite large. Up the neck, at the second octave (15th fret) it's much easier. Remember, these are moveable shapes. If this was on the 4th fret of the *A* string, it would be a *C#* major arpeggio. If it were on the 5th fret of the *A* string, it would be a *D* major arpeggio, and so on.

The arpeggio doesn't need to start on the 1, end on the 1, or be in order. That is just the way that most guitarists play them. You can try playing this arpeggio starting on the *E* or *G* if you like.

Arpeggios can be *A* minor shaped as well. These look like the open *A* minor chord. I will add the extra note to the *A* minor chord shape to make it follow 1-b3-5. In *C* this would be *C-Eb-G*.

TAB 7-2 illustrates the basic *A* minor shaped arpeggio. The arpeggio is a *C* minor.

Tab 7-2:

The next arpeggio shape is the *D* shape. This is the most used shape. It's called the *D* shape because it coincides with the *D* open chords, such as *D* major, *D* minor, etc. The *D* shape is a bit different than the *A* shape because the *D* shape appears to be different than the normal *D* chord that we play every day. In actuality, it looks more like a *C* chord than a *D* chord, but alas I didn't name it. The following chords are in the *D* shape. Note the 1st chord is a standard *D* and the 2nd one is the *D* shape arpeggio form.

Tab 7-3:

TAB 7-3 shows the *C* major arpeggio in the *D* shape. The second *C* major arpeggio is an octave higher. This form as you can see ends on the *G* and not the *C*.

The D minor shaped arpeggios are next. Remember these arpeggios are in *C*.

Tab 7-4:

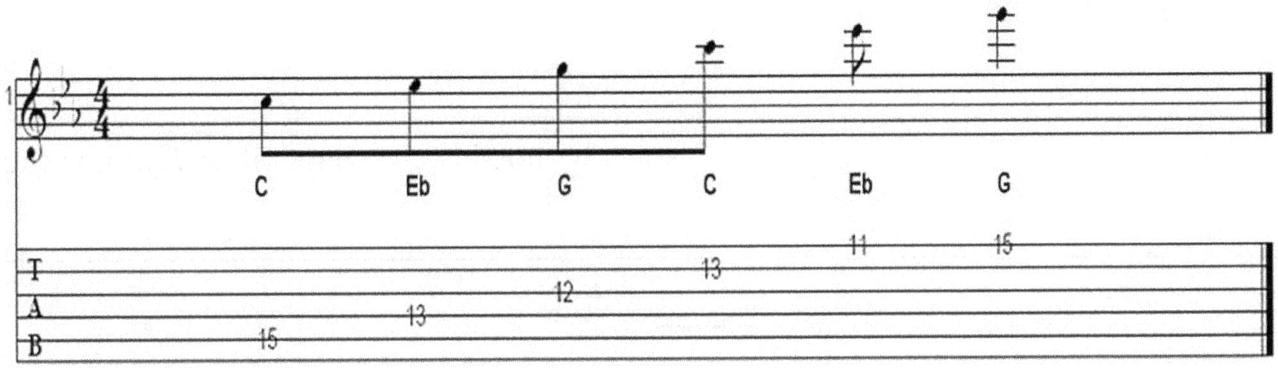

In TAB 7-4 the *Eb* would be below the open *E* string, so I only entered the TAB for the 2nd octave.

The last shape commonly used is the *E* shape. This is the least used of the three shapes shown here. The *E* shape coincides with the open *E* chords. These are not in the 1-3-5 form. They are in 1-5-1-3-5-1, so I will adjust it in the TAB.

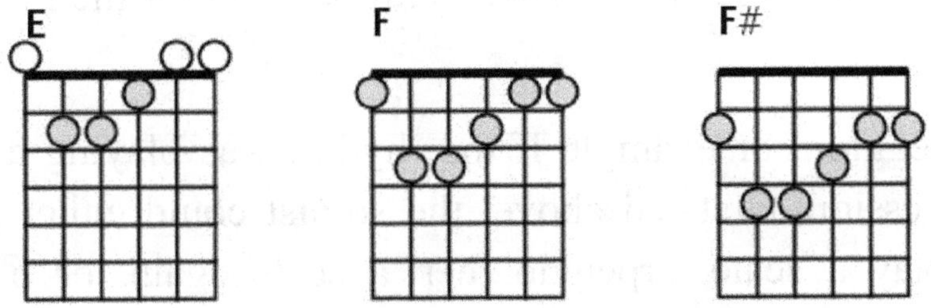

Tab 7-5:

The *E* minor shape is as you would expect by now, in the shape of an *E* minor chord.

Tab 7-6:

Now that we have the concept of what they are and what they look like, the obvious question is how they are used. An arpeggio can be used in many formats. If a chord progression of I-IV-V was being played in the key of C, then one could play the I arpeggio over the I chord to produce a melody over the chord. This could be done for the IV and V chords in the progression as well.

You could solo with an arpeggio. For example if the rhythm was playing a chord progression with the I-IV-V progression as stated above, the soloist could either play a scale and go into an arpeggio, play a scale, arpeggio then a scale again, or play all arpeggios over the chord progression.

Tab 7-7:

Tab 7-7 shows a scale-arpeggio-scale type of run that could be incorporated over a chord progression. Of course, this is just a basic run for information purposes. Notice the *C* major scale is not in order. A scale doesn't need to be played one note after the other and sound like a scale, although the last measure has the *C* major scale played backwards.

Tab 7-8 shows a vi-iii chord progression in the key of *C*. Guitar 2 plays an *A* minor arpeggio in 2 different octaves, the first being the *D* shaped and the second octave arpeggio is the bottom half of the *A*m shaped arpeggio form. The second measure plays the *E* shaped *E* minor arpeggio. Notice that the *E* minor arpeggio doesn't start on *E*, nor does it start on the *E* string. This arpeggio starts at the bottom half of the arpeggio and then works its way back up to the lower *E*.

Tab 7-8:

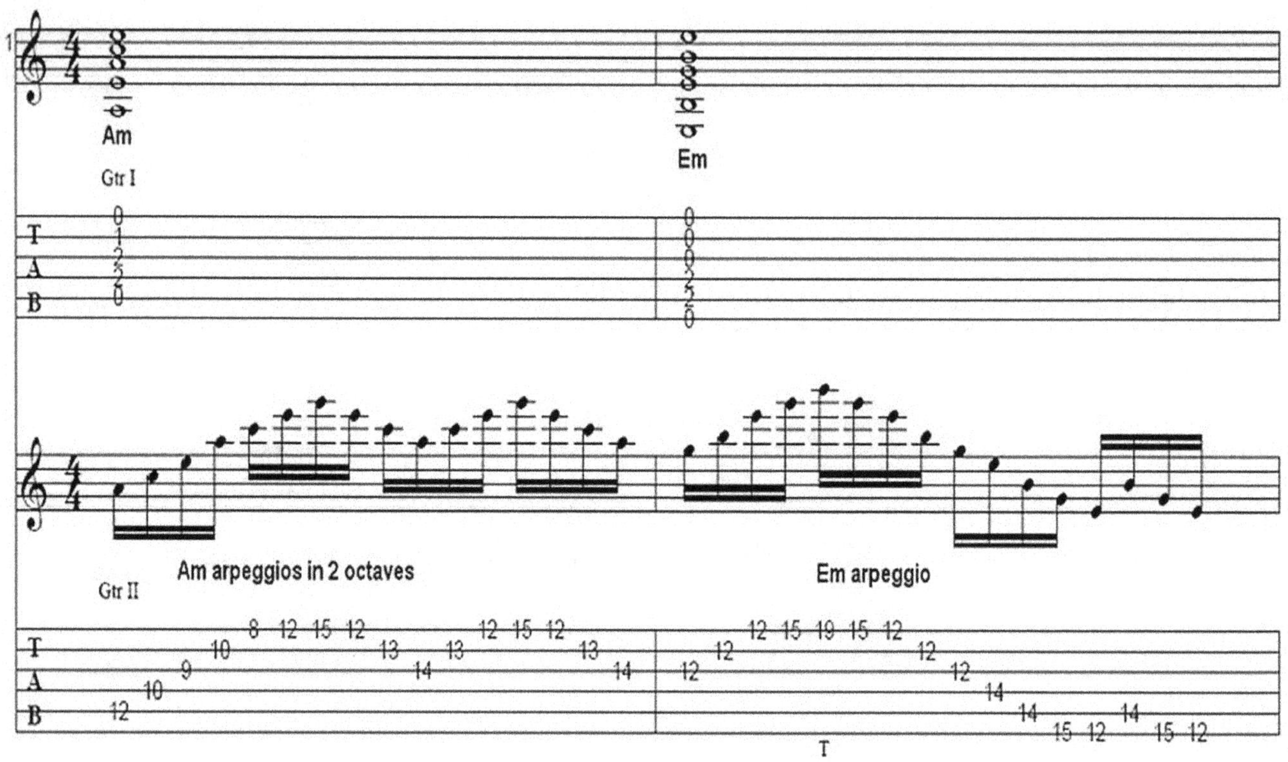

When playing arpeggios, play different ones back to back, like when you studied chords. Listen how they sound together. Try playing arpeggios in a key diatonically (I-ii-iii-IV-V-vi-vii). Then try playing in patterns. I like the pattern of 4ths. Here is an example that follows the pattern of 4ths.

Tab 7-9:

The pattern: ii-vi-I-iv

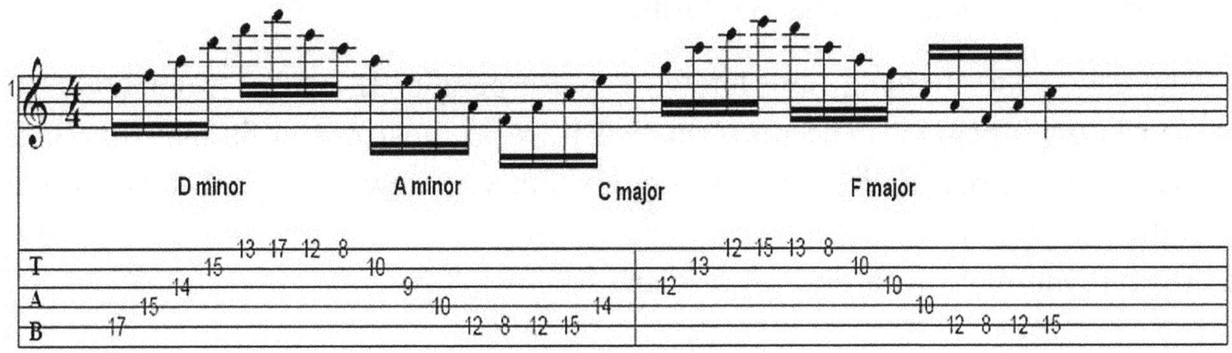

Tab 7-9: doesn't show the run I usually play because we haven't covered enough of the patterns to do so. But, it is a good example. Try thirds, sixths, etc. See what <u>you</u> like.

Tab 7-10:

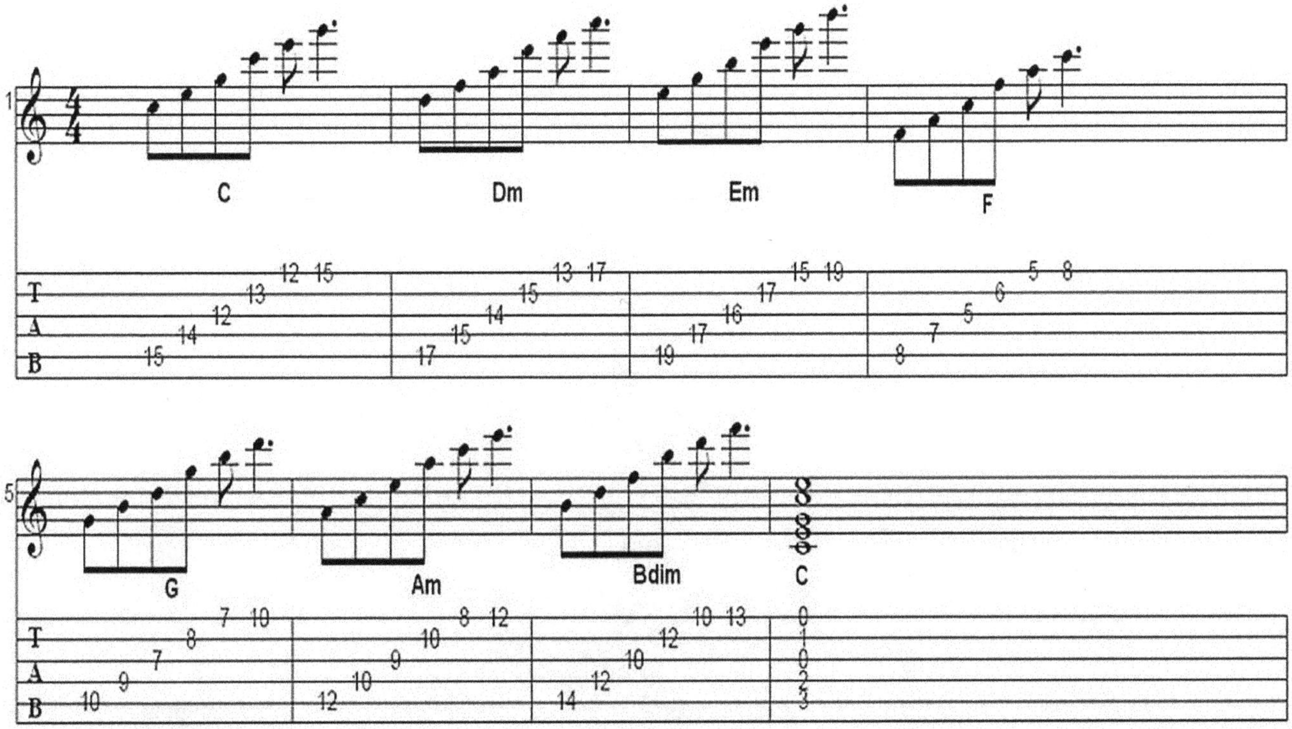

TAB 7-10 shows the diatonic arpeggios in the key of C. Note that these go exactly with the chords in the key of C. If the chords in a major scale are always M-m-m-M-M-m-d, then the arpeggios should be the same because an arpeggio is a broken chord. Keep it simple. Look for relationships and similarities.

There is a lot of stock, here lately, in the arpeggio. If you're "somebody" on the guitar you know arpeggios. The problem that I see in most people is that they spend so much time learning scales, licks, and arpeggios, but very few ever want to spend the time to learn the theory behind it. Understanding the theory behind the music allows you to be more creative, more intricate, and a musician.

Playing things at the speed of light can be cool here and there, but creating melodies is much harder. When every note is 16ths or 32ths all you hear is the progression of the scale or arpeggio. When you have notes with longer and shorter times, rests between notes, bends, slides, staccato, accentuation, etc. You utilize music to its fullest. When you play a scale as fast as you can, you sound boring.

Take the time to think of the chords being arpeggiated and the underlying chord that is being played.

Chapter 8 – Suspended 2nd & 4th Arpeggios

The Arpeggio Introduction chapter contained an excerpt from my book *A Guitarist's Guide to Theory*. It is a generalized book that covers a large amount of information in a short amount of time. The other books, like this one, go in depth on a subject.

We now will spend some more time looking at different arpeggios, where we can use them, and how to mix them in with what we are working with.

The basic arpeggios, as described in the previous chapter, are derivatives of the "cowboy chords". I will try to insert chord diagrams, and then tab to show the forms.

Let's recap the basics:

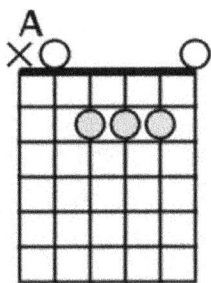

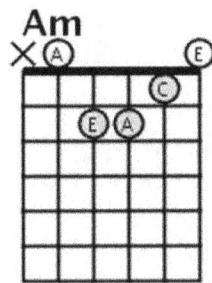

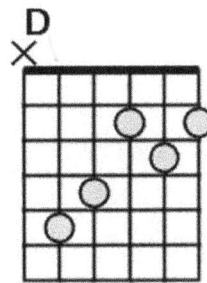

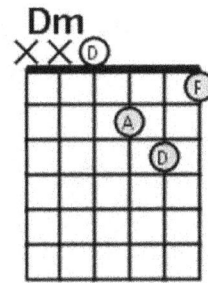

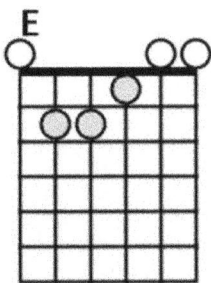

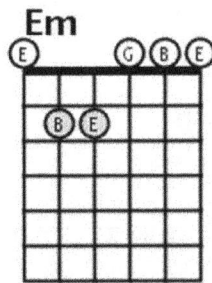

Tab 8-1: Basic arpeggio shapes

Tab 8-1 shows the basic forms, or shapes, of the arpeggios. When playing any major or minor chord, they will all follow this progression down the neck, in shape. Then they start back over on the 1st shape, i.e. F major starts with the E form on the 1st fret, the next form is the D form on the 8th fret, then there is the A form on the 8th fret, and we start back over at the E form on the 13th fret.

On Tab 8-1 we can see the A form, to the E form, and then the D form. The next, in order of succession, form to be played out of these basic shapes would be the A form at the 15th fret. Learn the major and minor basic forms in order.

These basic shapes will be the foundation for the rest of the arpeggios. If you don't have these memorized or have a good understanding about what we are doing; it would be a good idea to get that under your belt before moving on.

SUSPENDED 2nd and 4th

Many of the exotic scales that we went over had jacked up triads and it made more sense to use suspended chords. You can see this by thumbing through the short list of recommended chords at the end of each scale example. If you wanted to use the exotic scales, these suspended arpeggios would come in handy.

The idea of a suspended chord is that there is no major or minor character. This is because the 3rd of the scale is missing and either a 2nd or 4th interval is inserted in its place.

I usually teach these by saying that the identity of the chord has been suspended. The real musical idea is that when going through a series of chords, one of the notes is carried over to the next chord, and then resolves on the following chord. The note carried over is suspended, and it must resolve downward.

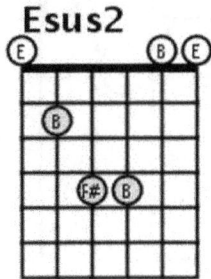

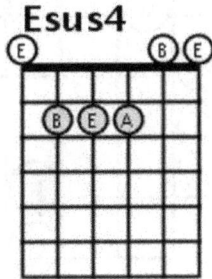

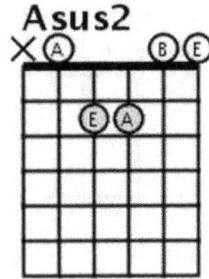

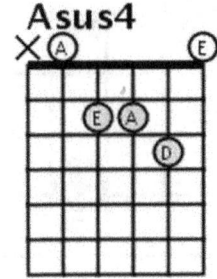

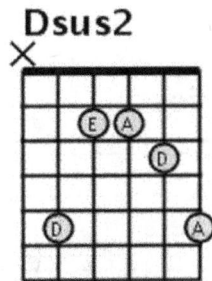

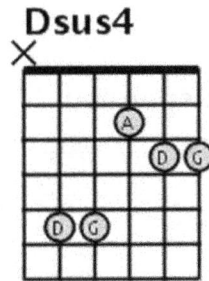

Esus2 **Esus4** **Asus2** **Asus4**

Dsus2 **Dsus4**

G Suspended 2nd

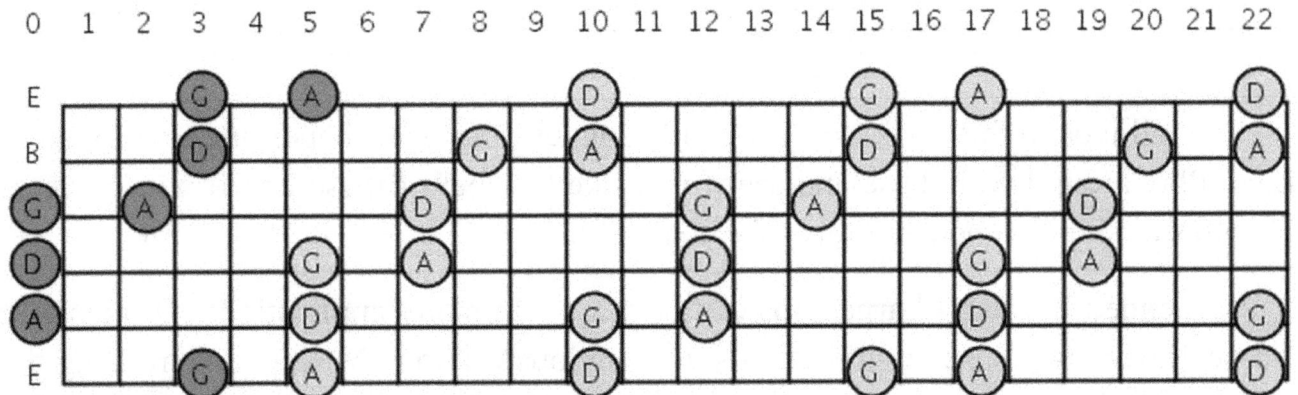

G Suspended 4th

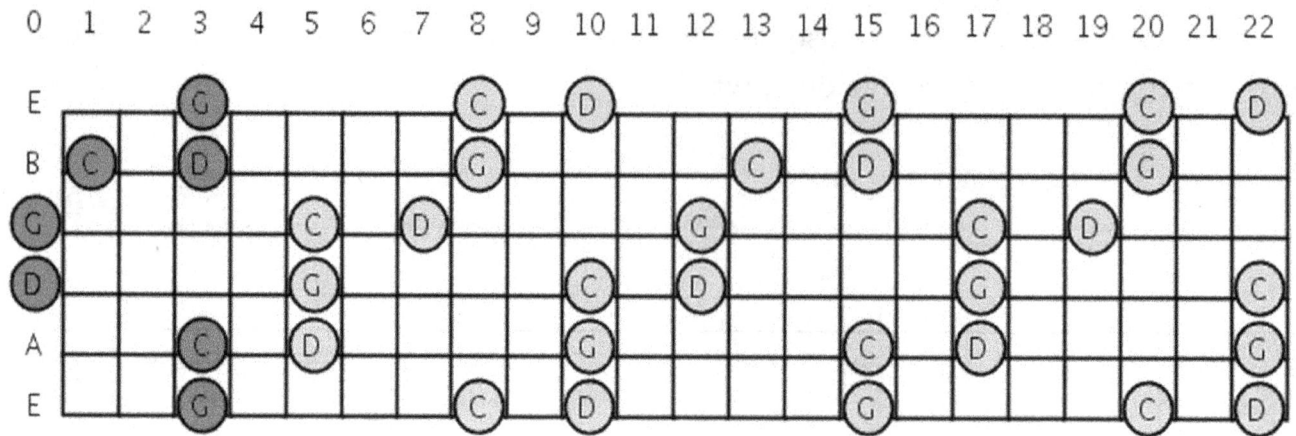

Fretboard diagram (frets 0–22), strings E B G D A E:

String	Notes (fret positions)
E	G(3), C(8), D(10), G(15), C(20), D(22)
B	C(1), D(3), G(8), C(13), D(15), G(20)
G	G(0), C(5), D(7), G(12), C(17), D(19)
D	D(0), G(5), C(10), D(12), G(17), C(22)
A	C(3), D(5), G(10), C(15), D(17), G(22)
E	G(3), C(8), D(10), G(15), C(20), D(22)

Tab 8-2: Suspended 2nd & Suspended 4th Arpeggios

```
        Gtr I  Gsus2 - E form   Gsus2 - D form   Csus2 - A form   Gsus4 - E form   Gsus4 - D form   Gsus4 - A form
T |-------------3------------------10---------------1015----------------3------------------810----------------1015----|
A |-------3------------------8-10------------10------------------3------------------8------------------13-----|
  |----2--------------7-----------------12-------------------5----------------7-----------------12-----------|
  |--5-----------------7-----------------12-------------------5---------------10----------------1012---------|
A |----5--------------5-10-----------1012---------------35----------------10-----------------10--------------|
B |--3-5----------5-10-----------10-12--------------3--------------------10-----------------10--------------|
              3
```

Like all tabs in this book; these are only suggestions. The shapes are how I would play them. Play around with these and see if you like the feel of these and if not, move one of the notes or skip that note entirely, if you have to.

Suspended 2nd and 4th arpeggios can be played in many applications. Of course, these can be played over sus2 or sus4 chords; too obvious, I know. Most people reading this are going to be playing over power chords, so the possibility of dissonance won't be an issue.

Because of the idea of resolution in the suspension; try playing a suspended arpeggio and then resolving it to the major, i.e. A-Asus-A, Asus4-A, or Asus2-A-Asus4.

Tab 8-3: A suspended arpeggio resolved example

By leaving the key signature of Tab 8-4 in C, you can see that only the A major arpeggio section has the C# in it. The Asus2 is A-B-E and the Asus4 is A-D-E.

An interesting thing to note is the 1st inversion of the Asus4 chord is D-E-A (Dsus2) and Asus4 is the 2nd inversion of Dsus2. So, Asus2 is the 2nd inversion of Esus4. So, sus4 chords are inversions of sus2 chords and sus2 chords are inversions of sus4 chords.

Chapter 9 – M7, m7, dom7, & m(M7) Arpeggios

MAJOR 7th, MINOR 7th, DOMINANT 7th, and MINOR(MAJOR 7th)

The major 7th (M7) chord is a major chord with a major seventh added to it. That means that you have a major triad consisting of the root, M3, P5 and on top of that you add the M7 interval, i.e., CM7: C-E-G-B.

The minor 7th (m7) chord is a minor chord with a minor seventh added to it. This would be a minor triad consisting of the root, m3, P5, and then you add the m7 interval, i.e., Cm7: C-Eb-G-Bb.

The dominant 7th, e.g., C7, chord is a major chord with a minor seventh added to it. This is a major triad consisting of the root, M3, P5 and lastly you add the m7 interval, i.e., C7: C-E-G-Bb.

The minor(Major 7), e.g., Cm(M7), is a minor chord with a major seventh added to it. That means you have a minor triad consisting of a root, m3, P5 and then add a M7 interval, i.e., Cm(M7): C-Eb-G-B.

We will look at the chords as they are in all three base shapes/forms ; the E, A, and D. Creativity is the key to all arpeggios. Just like the previous chords and arpeggio examples, there are virtually infinite ways to make these, but I will give some realistic, functional examples that you can jump in and use immediately.

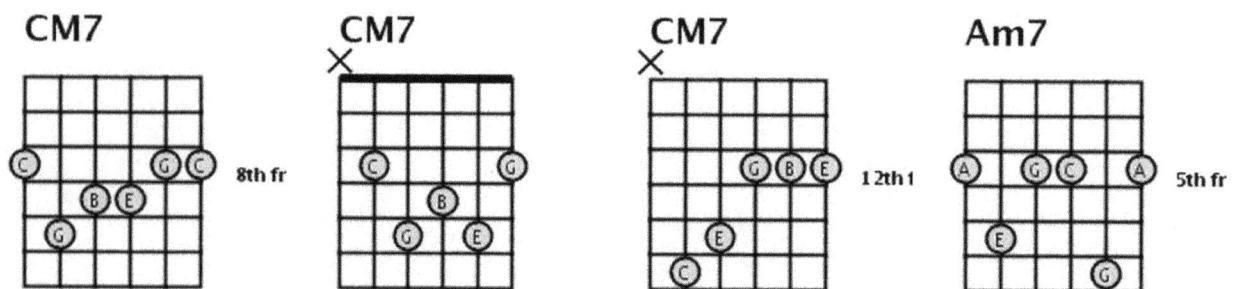

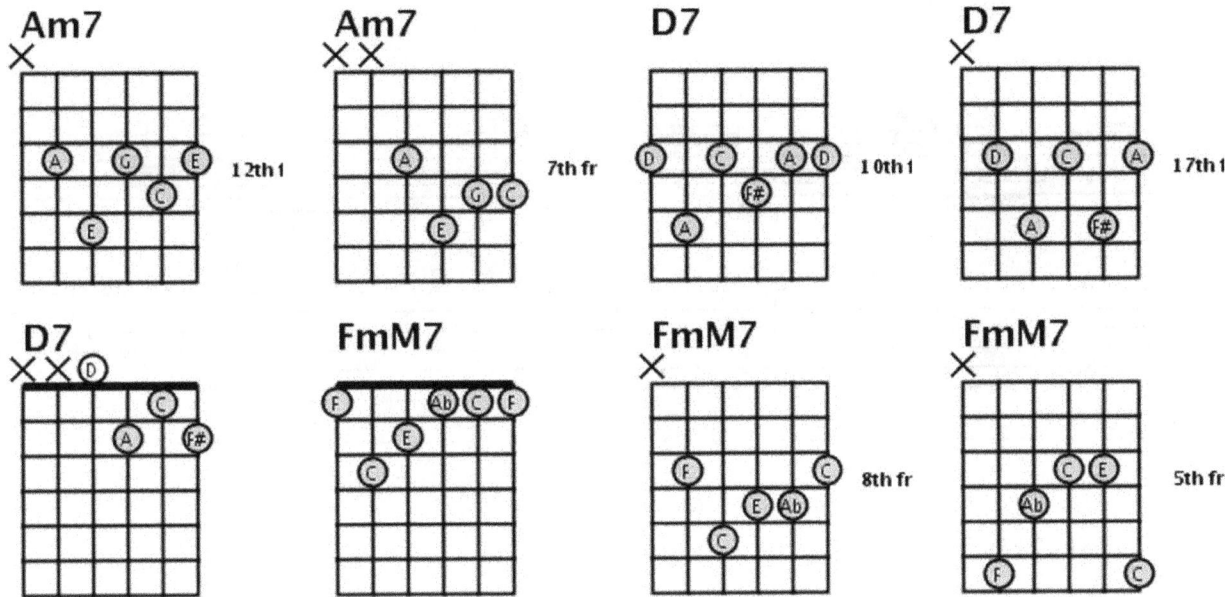

The chords above are in the three base forms, the E, A and D shapes. I could have had the E shape an E chord, the A shape an A chord, and the D shape a D chord, but we don't need to look at them like this. We should look at the shapes like forms and know all three forms for each chord.

C Major 7th

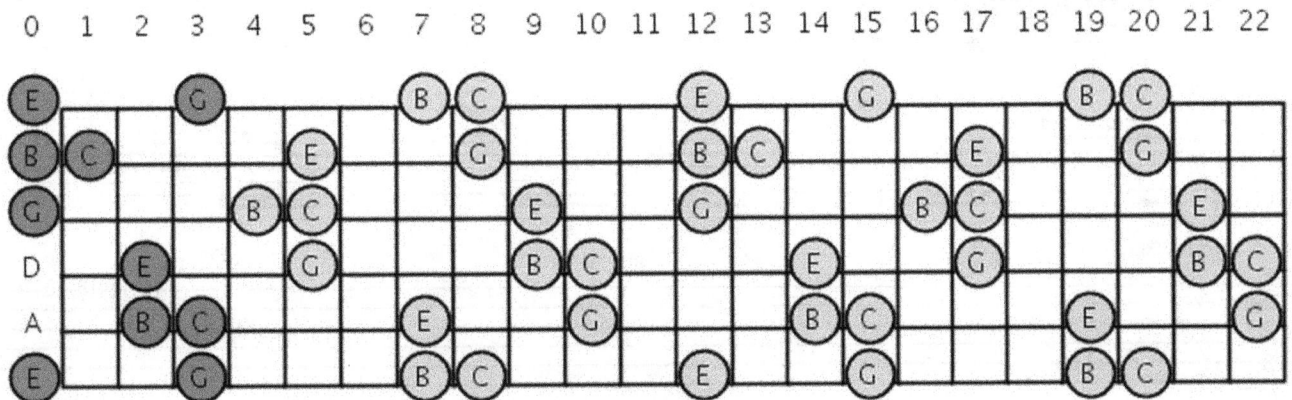

Tab 9-1: CM7 arpeggios

GtrI   CM7 - E form   CM7 - A form   CM7 - D form

C Minor 7th

| 0 | 1 | 2 | 3 | 4 | 5 | 6 | 7 | 8 | 9 | 10 | 11 | 12 | 13 | 14 | 15 | 16 | 17 | 18 | 19 | 20 | 21 | 22 |

E   G   Bb   C   Eb   G   Bb   C
B C   Eb   G   Bb   C   Eb   G
G G   Bb   C   Eb   G   Bb   C   Eb
D Eb   G   Bb   C   Eb   G   Bb   C
A Bb C   Eb   G   Bb   C   Eb   G
E   G   Bb   C   Eb   G   Bb   C

Tab 9-2: Cm7 arpeggios

GtrI   Cm7 - E form   Cm7 - A form   Cm7 - D form

C 7th

Tab 9-3: C7 arpeggios

C Minor Major 7th

Tab 9-4: Cm(M7) arpeggios

The major 7th arpeggios (Tab 9-1) can be used over the I or IV chords in any major key progression or the III or VI chords in any minor key progression. The major seventh can be inserted into solos mixing the Ionian mode→M7 arpeggio and Lydian→M7 arpeggio.

The minor 7th arpeggios (Tab 9-2) can be used over any ii, iii, and vi chords in any major key progression or the i, iv, and v chords in any minor key progression. The minor seventh can be inserted into the solos mixing the Dorian mode→m7 arpeggio, Phrygian mode→m7 arpeggio, and Aeolian mode→m7 arpeggio.

The dominant 7th arpeggios (Tab 9-3) can be used over any V chord in any major key progression or the VII chord in any minor key progression.

The minor(Major 7th) arpeggios (Tab 9-4) can be used over the i chord in the Harmonic minor progression or any of the other m(M7) chords derived from odd scales like the exotic scales in the chapters above.

Tab 9-5: CM7 arpeggio phrase

Tab 9-5 shows a phrase that goes from an Ionian mode, to a CM7 arpeggio, back to an Ionian mode, then lastly to another CM7 arpeggio.

Tab 9-6: Cm7 arpeggio phrase

Tab 9-7: C7 arpeggio phrase

Tab 9-7 is F Ionian, which is to say, C Mixolydian. This phrase uses two forms of the C7 arpeggio, the C Mixolydian and F Ionian to make a quick fluid movement up and then down the fretboard.

Tab 9-8: Cm(M7) arpeggio phrase

Tab 9-8 uses the Cm(M7) arpeggio. This has a M7 like the C Harmonic minor. The phrase above uses the C Harmonic minor and the Cm(M7) arpeggio. Notice the key signature is Cm. As stated in the Harmonic minor chapter, the Harmonic minor shares the same key signature as the Cm, allowing for the naturals in the notation.

Chapter 10 – Diminished 7th & m7b5 Arpeggios

What most people call a diminished chord is actually a half diminished chord. A diminished chord is 1-b3-b5-bb7, whereas a half diminished is 1-b3-b5-b7. There are two different diminished scales, the whole-half and the half-whole. This means that one scale is W-H-W-H-W-H-W-H and the other is H-W-H-W-H-W-H-W.

DIMINISHED 7TH ARPEGGIOS

A Diminished Whole Half

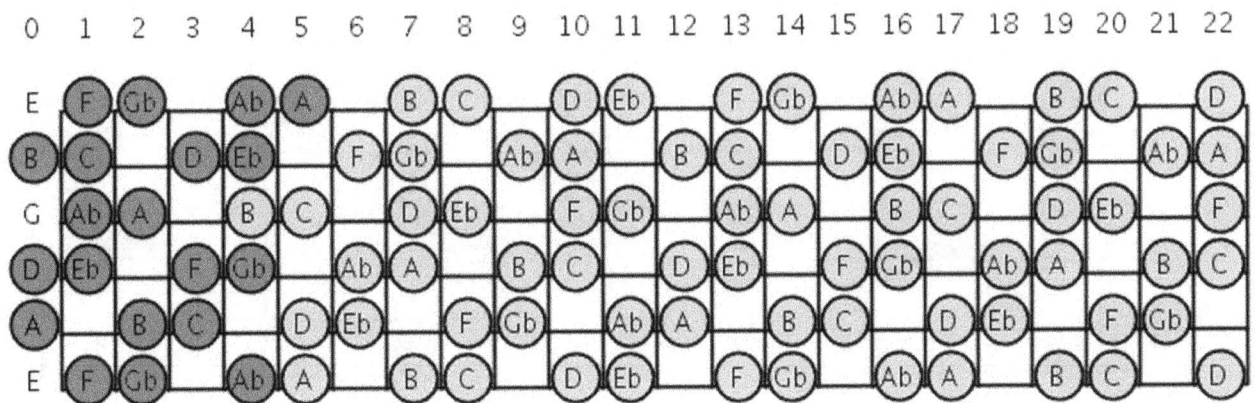

A Diminished Half Whole

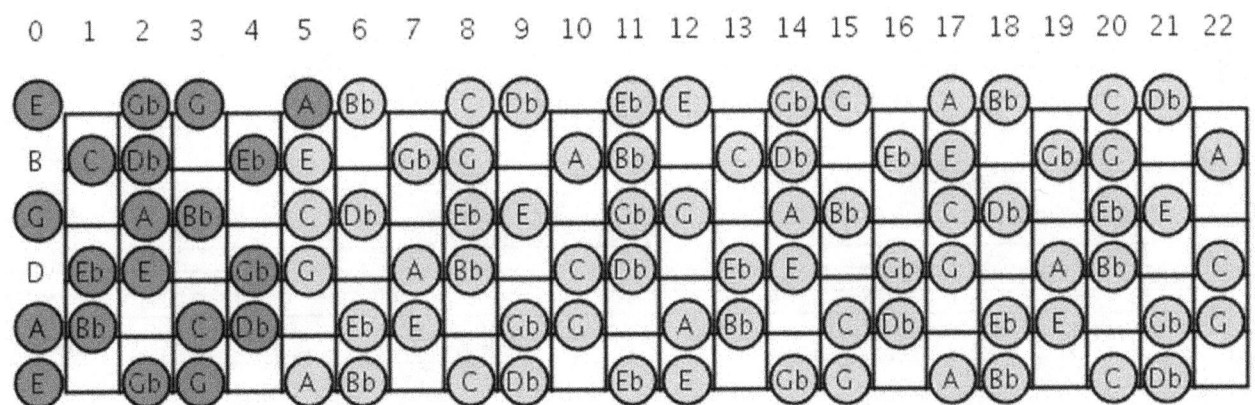

In the key of A, the diminished is A-C-D#, yielding 1-b3-b5. This is the signature for a diminished chord. The diminished 7th chord is A-C-D#-F#, giving us 1-b3-b5-bb7. Major scales do NOT have dim7 chords in their progressions. They have m7b5 chords (half diminished). In the key of Bb major, A diminished is A-C-D#, but the seventh chord is A-C-D#-G.

So, when playing diminished arpeggios, it's good to know that you are adding in that bb7, which needs to be considered.

There are only three diminished scales. If we have A-Bb-C-Db-Eb-E-Gb-G, the A diminished half whole scale, because it's a symmetrical scale, you can start it on any note before a half step. You can do this only three times before you run into the first scale.

A Diminished 7th

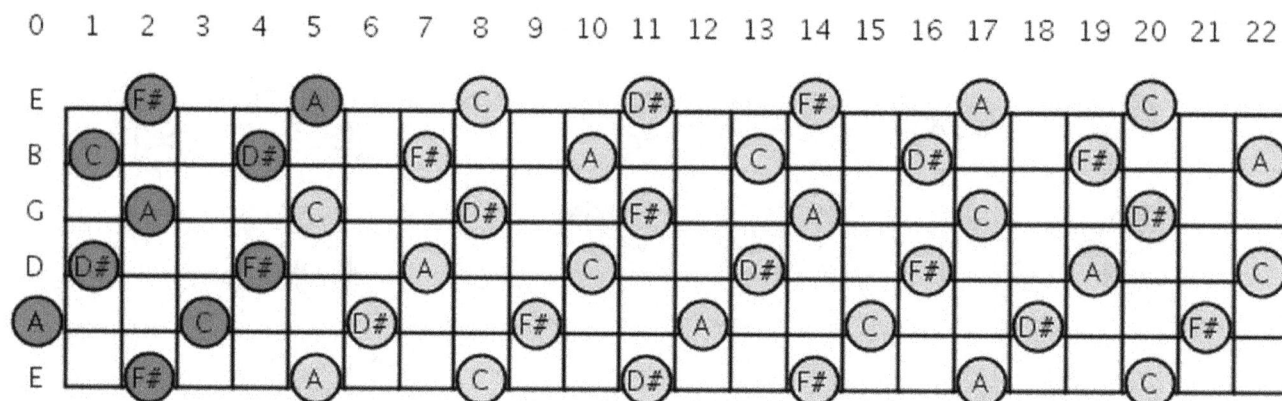

Tab 10-1: A diminished arpeggio backwards

Tab 10-2: A diminished arpeggio long

Tab-10-3: A diminished arpeggio short

I usually play the diminished arpeggio three different ways, backwards, long and short. The backwards scale is obvious when you play it. The long and short versions are not much different from each other, but the names gave me a way to tell them apart when teaching them.

Tab 10-4:

Tab 10-4 goes down A diminished arpeggio long form and then back up A diminished arpeggio short version. If you go back forward, you would be playing the first inversion of the original arpeggio.

Tab 10-5:

Tab 10-5 goes down A diminished arpeggio long and then back up A diminished arpeggio backwards. If you went back down, you would be playing the second inversion of the original arpeggio.

Diminished arpeggios can be used over a dominant 7 chord. The B7 chord is B-D#-F#-A and the D# diminished arpeggio is D#-F#-A-C. You should notice that they share 3 of the same notes. The F# diminished arpeggio is F#-A-C-D#, A diminished arpeggio is A-C-D#-F#, and obviously the C diminished arpeggio is C-D#-F#-A. They all are the same diminished scale starting on different degrees (no pun intended), thus they all share 3 notes with the dom7 chord.

Tab 10-6: F# diminished arpeggio over B7

Tab 10-6 shows an example of playing an F# diminished arpeggio over a B7 chord.

Many guitarists in the neoclassical guitar genre play the diminished arpeggio alongside the harmonic minor or the Phrygian dominant scales. Many times this is done by playing off of the seventh of the harmonic minor (G#°7) and letting it resolve up into the A. The 5th chord is the E7 (E-G#-B-D) or E7b9 (E-G#-B-D-F#). The G# diminished arpeggio is G#-B-D-F# sharing all but the E of the E7b9 chord.

Tab 10-7: G# diminished arpeggios to E Phrygian dominant

Tab 10-7 shows a G# diminished arpeggio played over an E7b9 chord, then an E Phrygian dominant is played over an Am chord.

The diminished is a really good chord to resolve one half step up. Tab 10-7 is playing off of the G# diminished arpeggio, resolving to the I, even though the chord progression is V-I.

m7b5 ARPEGGIOS

Interestingly enough, the m7b5 is not used as much as it should be. Many use the diminished arpeggio thinking that the seventh chord in the major scale is a diminished 7th, not knowing that it is really half diminished.

The m7b5 arpeggio can be used in many of the ways that the diminished can be used. The difference is that it contains all of the notes of the major scale and doesn't have any notes to be careful that are out of key.

This makes it easier to use than the diminished and is the same idea as using a Locrian mode.

B Minor 7th Flat 5th

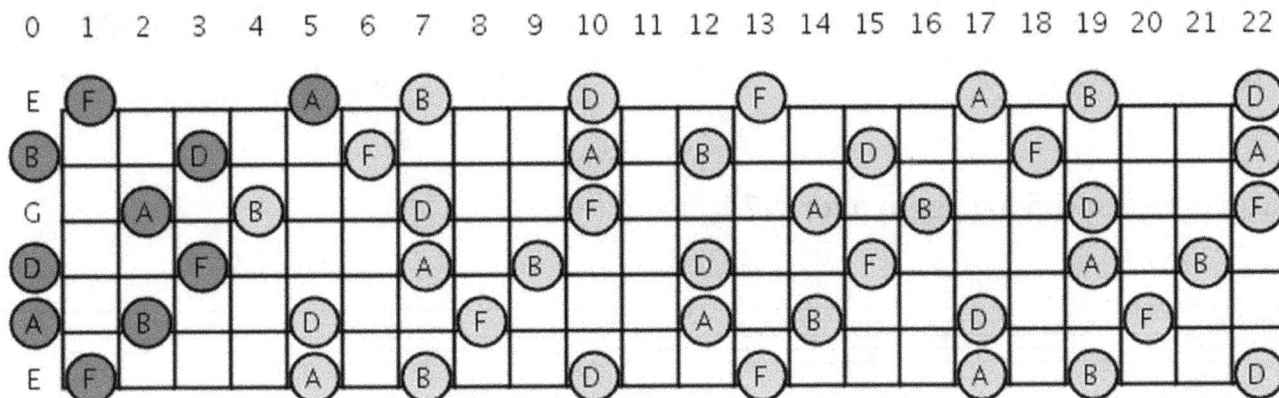

Tab 10-8: Bm7b5 arpeggio

Tab 10-8 uses the same second measure as Tab 10-7, but the first measure has the Bm7b5 arpeggio over a Bm7b5 chord. The arpeggio resolves on the I as before, but is a more straight forward vii-I resolution than the diminished example.

You can also use the same concept as before, with the diminished, by playing the m7b5 arpeggio over the V chord. Using the key of C again we get the Bm7b5 arpeggio over a G7 chord. G7 is G-B-D-F and the Bm7b5 is B-D-F-A. The vii is a substitution chord for the V chord for the same reason that we play the vii arpeggio over the V chord; they share three of the four notes, B-D-F.

Tab 10-9: Bm7b5 arpeggio over G7

Tab 10-9 plays a Bm7b5 over a G7 chord and then resolving to the I, the C major. The C major arpeggio is played over the I chord.

The m7b5, like the diminished arpeggio can be used as a transition chord, too. You could play them in between other arpeggios that *are* in the scale. An example of this would be playing I-biiº-ii-biiiº-iii-V-I.

Tab 10-10: m7b5 as passing arpeggios

Tab 10-10 plays the m7b5 arpeggios as passing arpeggios (chords) in between the chords in the key of C, as described in the previous paragraph. I usually use diminished as opposed to half diminished, but they can be used in the same respect.

Chapter 11 –Arpeggio Additions

This chapter is a non-exhaustive look at adding to base and seventh arpeggios. The concept and some examples will be given, but the idea is to learn the basic ones and to try to add to them in a way that you want. Just mimicking the examples in this and other books will never give you as much as experimenting on your own.

ADD 9 ARPEGGIOS

If there was any arpeggio besides the base arpeggio that I play, it's the add9 arpeggio. The idea is that we add the 2nd on the second octave, making a 9th. We usually call this a 2nd or sus2 when there is no 3rd interval. The makeup of these arpeggios is 1-3-5-9 or the minor would be 1-b3-5-9. In the key of C (Tab 11-1) and Am (Tab 11-2) it would be C-E-G-D or A-C-E-B, respectively.

C Major Add 9th

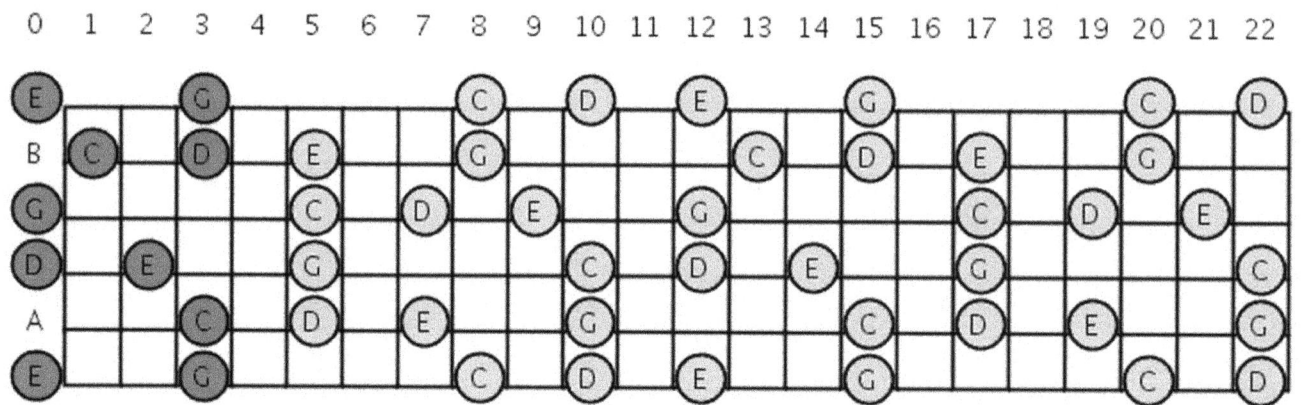

Tab 11-1:

A Minor 9th

The above arpeggio diagram includes the m7 (G). Disregard this note when playing the add 9.

Tab 11-2:

M6th & m6th ARPEGGIOS

The 6th arpeggios are like the add9 arpeggios, but you add a 6th to the triad instead of the 9th. The spellings of these arpeggios are 1-3-5-6 or the minor would be 1-b3-5-6. In the key of C (Tab 11-3) and Am (Tab 11-4) it would be C-E-G-A or A-C-E-F#, respectively. The Am6 is from the A melodic minor scale (ascending).

C 6th

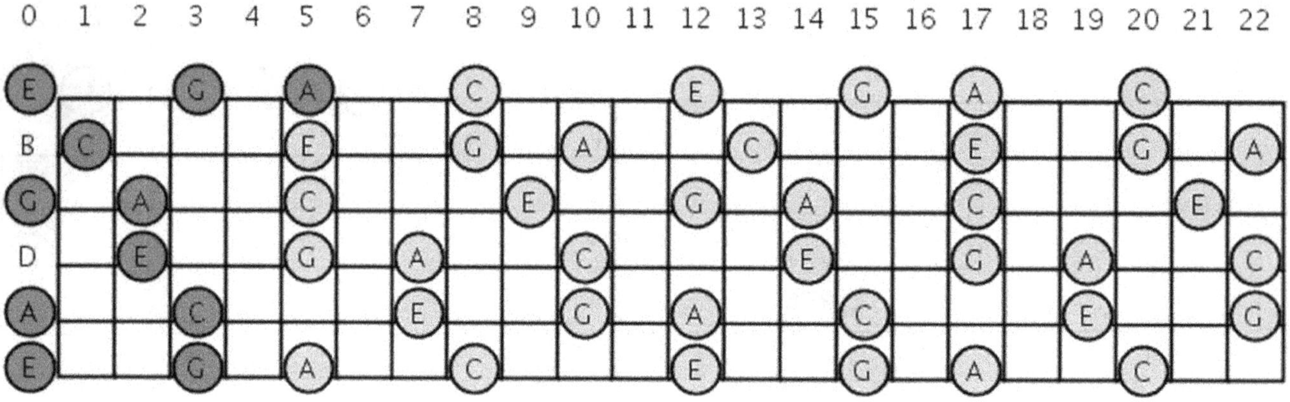
0 1 2 3 4 5 6 7 8 9 10 11 12 13 14 15 16 17 18 19 20 21 22
B
D

Tab 11-3:

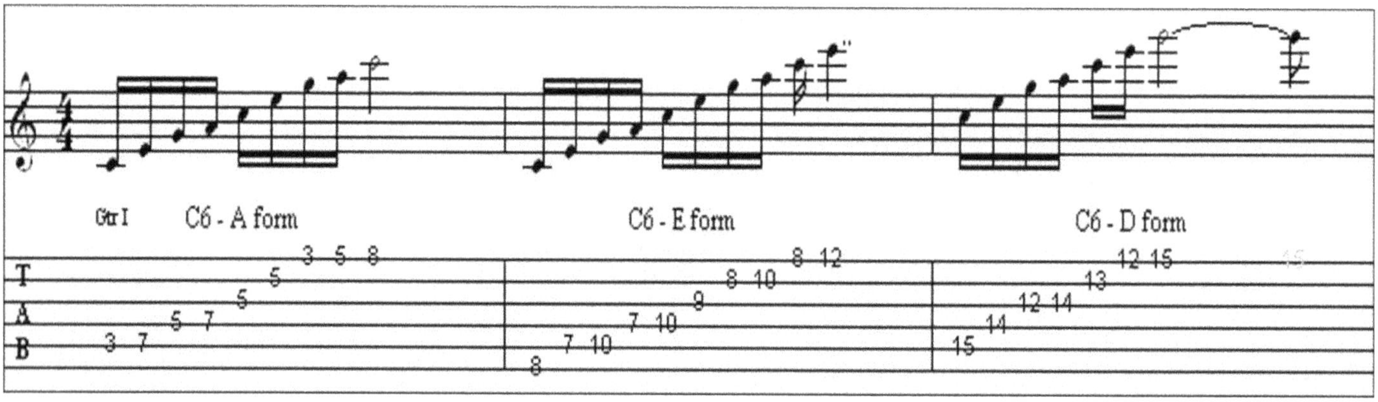
Gtr I
C6 - A form
C6 - E form
C6 - D form
T
A
B

A Minor 6th

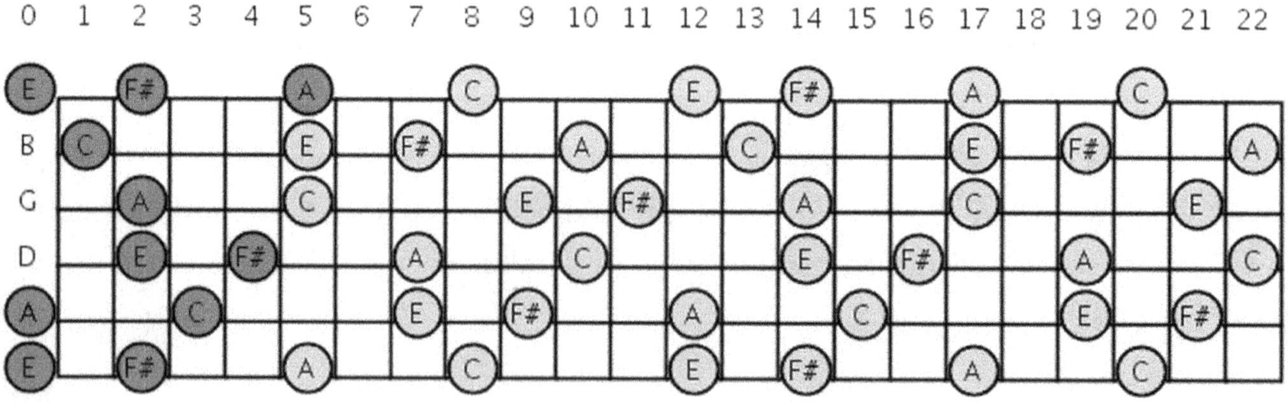
0 1 2 3 4 5 6 7 8 9 10 11 12 13 14 15 16 17 18 19 20 21 22
B
G
D

Tab 11-4:

M6 add9 & m6 add9 ARPEGGIOS

Here is something that will be easy to remember. The M6 add9 is the same as a major pentatonic scale. The m6 add9 does not look like the minor pentatonic though. The spellings of these are as follows: M6 add9 – 1-3-5-6-9, m6 add9 – 1-b3-5-6-9. The CM6 add9 (also written C6/9) is C-E-G-A-D, and the Am6 add9 (also written Am6/9) is A-C-E-F#-B.

C 6th Add 9th

Tab 11-5:

Gtr I C6/9 - A form   C6/9 - E form   C6/9 - D form

A Minor 6th Add 9th

Tab 11-6:

Gtr I Am6/9 - A form   Am6/9 - E form   Am6/9 - D form

AUGMENTED ARPEGGIOS

The augmented arpeggio is one that can be added to many of the exotic scales in the previous chapters, such as the harmonic minor. It is built 1-3-#5, for example the C+ arpeggio is C-E-G#.

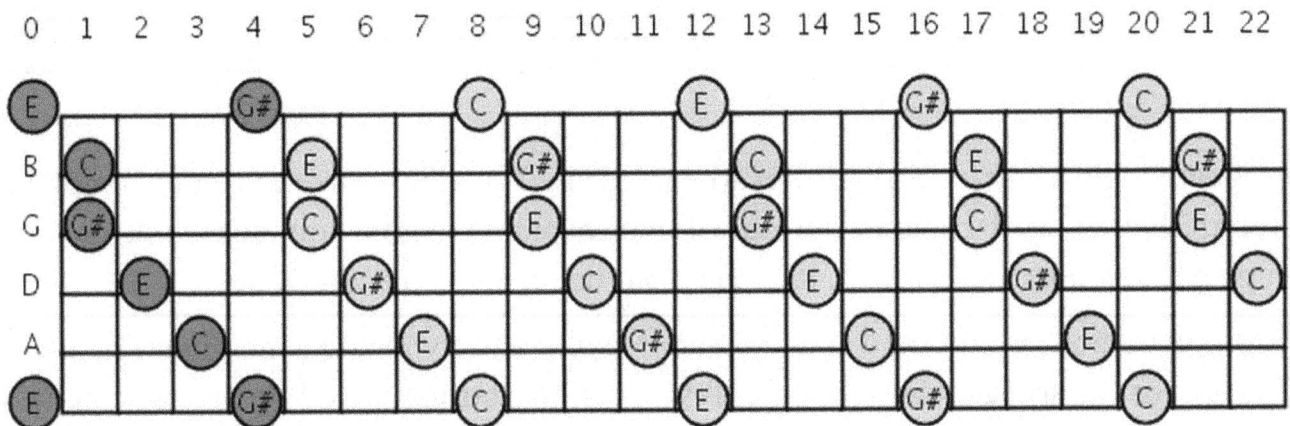

Tab 11-7:

Add#11 ARPEGGIOS

The add#11 arpeggios have a nice Asian sound and can be used alongside the Lydian mode (1-2-3-#4-5-6-7). The add#11 intervals are 1-3-#4-5, an example is C add#11 which is 1-3-5-#11 (also written 1-3-#4-5 or 1-3-b5-5).

Tab 11-8:

I could add another thirty-eleven arpeggios and I'm sure someone would complain that I forgot the sus2 #4 b13add9. The idea of this chapter is to give you ideas to be creative in playing arpeggios; add a 7 here, take the 3 out there, add a 6 and a 9, put in a 13, etc.

Look at the scales or mode that you are playing and try to add something like the m7b5 arpeggio or C+ arpeggio into the mix. Try not to be a boring, dwell on the same pentatonic for a month and add an arpeggio in the wrong key, kind of guy. Take your time, use your brain, and above all… have fun.

ABOUT THE AUTHOR

Bryan DeLauney lives in a small town in Alabama where he resides with his lovely wife, Kristen, and their wily cats. He has a degree in chemistry and works in petroleum blending and distribution. Bryan posts online guitar instructions and ideas on YouTube at
http://www.youtube.com/user/delauney
Enjoy playing guitar and God Bless!!